TIME, TALENT, AND TREASURE

TIME, TALENT, AND TREASURE

Reflections on the
U.S. Bishops' Model
for Parish Stewardship

C. Justin Clements

Liguori
LIGUORI, MISSOURI

Imprimi Potest:
Thomas D. Picton, C.Ss.R.
Provincial, Denver Province
The Redemptorists

Published by Liguori Publications
Liguori, Missouri
www.liguori.org

Library of Congress Cataloging-in-Publication Data

Clements, C. Justin, 1938–
     Time, talent, and treasure : reflections on the U.S. Bishops' model for parish stewardship / C. Justin Clements.—1st ed.
          p. cm.
     ISBN 978-0-7648-1500-3 (pbk.)
     1. Catholic Church—Finance. 2. Christian giving—Catholic Church. 3. Stewardship, Christian—Catholic Church. I. Title.
BX1950.C54 2006
248'.6088282—dc22   2006011200

Liguori Publications, a nonprofit corporation, is an apostolate of the Redemptorists. To learn more about the Redemptorists, visit *Redemptorists.com.*

Printed in the United States of America
12 11 10   6 5 4 3

Contents

What Is This Thing Called Stewardship?

Overview of Christ-centered stewardship, stewardship defined, and the benefits of these reflections. Each of the seven chapters begins with a portion of the text of the United States Conference of Catholic Bishops' pastoral letter: *Stewardship: A Disciple's Response, Tenth Anniversary Edition, 2002.*

The Turning Point • 6

There's a definite, palpable burst of insight in a Christian's life when stewardship becomes a way of life; some suggested resources.

Once More With Feelings • 9

Stewardship conversion involves an emotional as well as an intellectual response.

Am I Missing Something? • 10

Critical importance of a positive, joyful attitude among Christians engaged in stewardship conversion.

Two Little Words • 12

"I" and "stuff": we own nothing; everything really belongs to God.

Foreword

As we move through the beginning of the twenty-first century, the U.S. Catholic Church finds itself in a challenging position. Events such as the clergy sexual-abuse scandal and the increasing influence of secular values have put the Church on the defensive. We've seen important measures such as Mass attendance and financial contributions at all levels drift slowly downward. Clearly, we need a message of hope that will renew Catholics and reestablish our Catholic faith as the central part of our lives.

That message can be found in the message of stewardship. As Justin Clements so forcefully argues, stewardship is not fundraising. Rather, it is about a total way of life, about changing peoples' minds and hearts. It is about recognizing that all we have is really a gift from God, who asks us to return a portion in the form of our time, talent, and treasure to support God's work on earth. It is about developing a need to give rather than merely giving to a need. It is asking ourselves, "What do we own, and what owns us?" Stewardship is not something that we do; it is about who we are. What better message could there be to deliver to Catholics who have been bombarded by recent negative images!

But the notion of stewardship is foreign to most Catholics. That is why we need men like Justin Clements. Justin not only practices stewardship in his own life but also works in the service of the Church by directly assisting parishes in introducing and maintaining stewardship, and by speaking at numerous parish and diocesan gatherings throughout North America. Justin also possesses another wonderful gift—the gift to inspire parishioners to follow a stewardship life through his writing.

Following on the heels of his very successful book *Stewardship: A*

Parish Handbook, which dealt primarily with the practicalities of introducing stewardship, Justin now gives us a different type of book. *Time, Talent, and Treasure* follows the same philosophy as his earlier book, but is targeted more directly to parishioners' minds and hearts. Taking the seven categories related to the process of stewardship conversion found in the appendix of the tenth anniversary edition of the U.S. bishops' letter *Stewardship: A Disciple's Response,* Justin has demonstrated the ability to provide valuable and understandable stewardship lessons. Through a series of brief vignettes he connects the seven categories that the bishops have identified to reality as it currently exists in most Catholic parishes today. In the process he has provided us with a valuable road map to changing parishioners' minds and hearts and revitalizing parish life in the United States today.

As you enjoy this inspirational book, I hope that you will take from it the wonderful underlying lesson of stewardship: Stewardship is a joyful approach to living one's life! Understanding that simple lesson will go a long way in helping you and your fellow Catholics to develop your parish into one that is clearly identified as a "Yes-Parish."

CHARLES E. ZECH
PROFESSOR OF ECONOMICS
VILLANOVA UNIVERSITY

Preface

Stewardship: A Disciple's Response was originally published by the United States Conference of Catholic Bishops in 1992. In 2002, they issued a tenth anniversary edition of that landmark document and added two helpful appendices: "Stewardship and Development in Catholic Dioceses and Parishes" and "Stewardship Resources." Section IV of appendix II is called "Promoting Gifts of Time, Talent, and Treasure to the Parish and Diocese: Seven Steps to Success." This three-page section briefly touches on seven broad categories related to the process of stewardship conversion. The space constraints that were probably placed on the authors of this section did not allow for much more than a cursory mention of a few of many topics that fall under each of their seven steps. My motivation for selecting and organizing the reflections for this book was based on the value of exploring more fully some of the elements and strategies of stewardship conversion that relate to each of those seven steps.

The previously published articles included in this book are based on more than two decades of working with stewardship devotees in my own diocese as well as with parishes and other dioceses throughout the United States and Canada. All of the basics of the stewardship conversion process for parishes have been covered in my second book, *Stewardship: A Parish Handbook*, which was published by Liguori Publications in 2002. However, issues and nuances around the topics of stewardship and discipleship constantly arise thanks to the boundless creativity of my professional colleagues throughout North America as well as the parish stewardship committees I am privileged to serve in my own diocese.

This book begins with an introductory essay on stewardship followed by seven chapters, one devoted to each of the seven steps that the authors introduced with these words:

> The mission and ministries of the Church in the United States require the personal participation in and financial support of the Catholic people. The following suggestions are intended as a seven-steps process (or checklist) to help bishops, pastors, and their staffs and volunteers successfully promote gifts of time, talent, and treasure to the parish and diocese in a manner consistent with the theology of stewardship and principles of effective development (page 59).

And they closed their remarks with this paragraph:

> The seven steps suggested here are not intended to be an exhaustive list of all of the programs or activities that are required for success in promoting gifts of time, talent, and treasure. However, the experience of parishes and dioceses in many different regions of the country shows that if these seven principles are honored, the Catholic people will respond generously to the invitation to participate in the mission and ministries of their Church (page 61).

Each of the following chapters begins with the original text of one of the seven steps to success from the tenth anniversary edition of the U.S. bishops' pastoral followed by several reflections about various aspects of that particular step.

Here are some who might benefit from these reflections:

- Bishops pursuing ways to incorporate the messages of their own stewardship pastoral into the life of their dioceses.
- Priests and deacons looking for homily ideas about stewardship and discipleship.
- Members of parish stewardship committees who are passionate about their efforts to lead their parishes to total stewardship.

- Religious educators (directors of religious education, catechists, and Catholic schoolteachers) hunting for helpful tips to spark student discussion and stewardship activities.
- Seminarians seeking greater knowledge and understanding of the significance of the North American stewardship conversion movement.
- Diocesan or parish lay leaders searching for personal spiritual growth and helpful ideas for stewardship-related projects.
- Christians who simply want support and encouragement for their private journeys toward a stewardship way of life.

Introduction
What Is This Thing
Called Stewardship?

Here's a headline you'll probably never see in a popular magazine or local newspaper: "Stewardship Renaissance Transforms American Catholic Church." However, thanks to the determined, prophetic leadership of countless bishops, priests, religious, and lay leaders throughout North America, the stewardship way of life that characterized early American Catholic communities has been making a powerful comeback.

The bishops of the United States acknowledged and embraced this resurgence with the publication of their 1992 pastoral letter, *Stewardship: A Disciple's Response*. This marvelously crafted document gave Catholic stewardship pioneers and their followers the theological and scriptural motivation to persevere in their efforts to create a total stewardship conversion within the North American Church. A copy of the bishops' pastoral letter, especially the tenth anniversary edition published in 2002, should be prominently displayed and systematically studied in every Catholic parish and institution.

In spite of the rapidly spreading stewardship conversion movement, the concept of stewardship and the practice of stewardship as a way of life are still unfamiliar terrain for most Catholics. Stewardship is often perceived as a "Protestant thing" or as nothing more than a euphemism for fundraising. Both of these perceptions are inaccurate. Whenever the concept of stewardship is introduced to Catholics—or indeed to any disciple of Jesus Christ—one must always begin with the assertion that being a good steward is a requirement. Here's what the U.S. bishops said:

> Stewardship is an expression of discipleship, with the power to change how we understand and live out our lives (page 1).

> Generous sharing of resources…is central to [stewardship's] practice, and church support is a necessary part of this. Essentially, it means helping the Church's mission with money, time, personal resources of all kinds. This sharing is not an option for Catholics who understand what membership in the Church involves. It is a serious duty. It is a consequence of the faith which Catholics profess and celebrate (pages 6–7).

> Becoming a disciple of Jesus Christ leads naturally to the practice of stewardship. These linked realities, discipleship and stewardship, then make up the fabric of a Christian life in which each day is lived in an intimate, personal relationship with the Lord (page 14).

The bishops defined a Christian steward as "one who receives God's gifts gratefully, cherishes and tends them in a responsible manner, shares them in justice and love with others, and returns them with increase to the Lord." What a magnificent confluence of words and phrases! What a world we could create if this definition described the lifestyle of every Christian! You see, we stewardship aficionados are absolutely convinced that the solution to most of humankind's troubles is the universal acceptance of Christocentric stewardship.

Here are a few additional observations to help introduce the reflections about stewardship that follow in this book:

- Our model for stewardship is none other than Jesus Christ. Yes, we believe that Jesus was the Messiah with a divine nature, but he was also a human immersed in a particular historical milieu. Catholics and others who are striving to be good stewards live in a real world with real people. Examples of stewardship in action can be found in every community and society.

Organized religion has no monopoly on what constitutes good stewardship. Anyone who is serious about Christian discipleship can spot good stewardship in many different disciplines, lifestyles, and professions. Just as Jesus used the "stuff" of his times and culture to formulate his message, so, too, can today's disciples of Jesus draw from their experiences to identify and help spread the message of good stewardship.

• Stewardship is not fundraising. Let's repeat that last phrase together: **"Stewardship Is Not Fundraising."** When a process of stewardship conversion is officially introduced in a parish or diocese, many parishioners inadvertently reach for their wallets or purses—not to open them, but to protect them! Stewardship initiatives are often perceived as nothing more than sneaky ways to reach deeper into the pockets of the faithful. This unfortunate perception often presents a significant challenge for those who are responsible for directing a stewardship conversion process. One way to meet the challenge head-on is by intentionally and systematically emphasizing the critical importance of the other two stewardship "T's": Time and Talent.

• Eternal salvation is certainly serious business. But we can't forget that our faith is an Easter faith. We Christians need to lighten up a bit. We could use more joy and celebration, and less lethargy and lamentation in our faith lives. Good humor and lighthearted spirits should be the rule, not the exception, for disciples of Jesus.

Finally, stewardship is all about recognizing God as the source of everything we have and are, accepting our accountability for God's gifts, expressing our gratitude for them, and returning a sacrificial portion to help build the kingdom on earth. As you read the following reflections, my hope is that you will increasingly feel the warmth of the stewardship fire that burns within the hearts and minds of an ever-widening circle of North American Catholic disciples of Jesus Christ. My prayer is that you will renew—or begin to experience—the liberating peace and unbridled joy that a total stewardship way of life offers, and share that good news with others.

STEP 1

Personal Witness

Since stewardship is a way of life, and not simply a program of Church support, the most important ingredient in any effort to encourage giving of time, talent, and treasure is the personal witness of individuals (clergy, religious, and lay) who have experienced a change of heart as a result of their commitment to stewardship. For this reason, parishes and dioceses are strongly encouraged to ground their stewardship and development programs in the personal witness of the bishop, pastor, parish or diocesan staff, and volunteers. An example of this type of personal witness would be for the presider at a liturgy to make a financial contribution or complete a commitment card for time, talent, or resources.

Parish stewardship programs currently in use in parishes and dioceses throughout the United States provide excellent examples of clergy and lay witness talks that can be offered during the liturgies leading up to a stewardship or commitment weekend. To ensure that stewardship is seen as more than simply the parish's annual giving program, witness talks on stewardship themes should also be offered at various times throughout the year. Similarly, diocesan annual giving programs and other diocesan events should include opportunities for personal witness on the part of the bishop and others to the importance of stewardship as a faith response. It is also important that parish leaders present the parish financial

report at a different time, preferably a few months prior to the sac-
rificial giving presentation.

STEWARDSHIP: A DISCIPLE'S RESPONSE (PAGE 59)

The Turning Point

When steam-powered locomotives ruled the rails, every railroad yard
had a roundhouse that contained a giant turntable. When an engine
reached the end of the line for each haul, it was necessary to turn it and
place it on one of the tracks that radiated from the roundhouse in preparation for its next trip.

Stewardship conversion could be described as a spiritual roundhouse.
We enter from one direction with certain beliefs and values, we spin on
a theological and scriptural turntable that reorients our lives as disciples
of Jesus Christ, and we emerge on a new track as responsible stewards of
God's many gifts.

What is the turning point for stewardship conversion? What happens in a Christian's spiritual roundhouse that causes him or her to have
a change of heart and embrace a stewardship way of life? The answers to
these questions are unique to every disciple of Jesus and are usually
multifaceted. For some, the conversion may be triggered by a single, life-
altering event such as a serious illness, making a Cursillo, the birth of a
child, the death of a loved one, or participating in a program like RE-
NEW or Christ Renews His Parish. For others, stewardship conversion
may be a slow, subtle change that occurs over time. Some may embrace
their reconstructed Christian persona joyfully and willingly; others may
be figuratively dragged, kicking and screaming, into a new dimension of
discipleship.

There is, however, one particular burst of insight that may be the
principal key that unlocks the stewardship message and compels Christians to build their lives around it: the acceptance of God as the source
of all that we are and have. At the moment disciples of Jesus Christ accept this core tenet of the Catholic faith, a profound, personal transfor-
mation takes place. Suddenly everything is seen as a gift, and the newly
converted-to-stewardship disciples feel a sense of liberation from the

clutter of this world. They also experience a wave of gratitude and personal peace which, in turn, spurs them to more generous sharing of their time, talent, and treasure.

Such was the experience of a dentist who recently returned from Central America where he spent six weeks using his medical skills as a volunteer among the poor. Before his trip, he considered himself to be a devout Christian and a pretty good steward of time, talent, and treasure. But his missionary experience forced him to reexamine his entire value system. The grateful, often tearful, response of the people he served changed his life forever. He returned to the States with a completely different outlook about the things many North Americans use to measure success: wealth, fame, and power. For him, life was no longer about accumulating more but about sharing more; it was not about grasping for "bigger and better," it was about appreciating God's great generosity. The simple act of fixing the teeth of poor Central Americans inspired the dentist to recognize the multitude of blessings God had showered on him and his family, and produced a true stewardship conversion in his heart.

Unfortunately, there are no self-help or how-to manuals (other than sacred Scriptures, of course) that describe how parish leaders can bring parishioners to a similar spiritual pivot point. Because the process of stewardship conversion involves much trial and error, parishes need to develop extensive menus of programs and services. Somewhere, within a wide array of engaging time and talent opportunities, individual parishioners may find the catalyst that opens those personal doors leading to their conversion.

The good news for parish and diocesan leaders is that no one is alone in this struggle. Hundreds of dioceses and parishes throughout the United States are facing the same challenges regarding stewardship conversion. Because many of them are experiencing great successes and are willing to share their stories, there's no need to reinvent the stewardship wheel. The question is: How does one gain access to the wealth of knowledge that is currently available?

One of the premier sources of stewardship information is the International Catholic Stewardship Council. In recent years, ICSC membership has burgeoned as stewardship conversion moves to the front burners of the U.S. Catholic Church. Among ICSCs many services is an exchange program that has created an active network of parishes and dioceses sharing stewardship information and materials. You can review the ICSCs full range of activities at its Web site: www.catholicstewardship.org.

Another excellent resource for stewardship information is the United States Conference of Catholic Bishops. Check out the Web site for this official Catholic association at www.usccb.org.

A third source of stewardship ideas and materials is often overlooked: your own parishioners. Many people travel to other parts of the United States for vacations, to visit relatives, or for business purposes. When such trips include a weekend, Catholics usually attend Mass and often discover other parish communities engaged in stewardship conversion. Encourage parishioners to be "stewardship travelers." Ask them to bring creative stewardship ideas back from their travels.

A fourth assortment of stewardship-related information is being produced by all of the major Catholic publishing houses. In 2000, for example, Liguori Publications published my book *Stewardship: A Parish Handbook*. The book is based on more than twenty-five years of professional fundraising and stewardship education experience and was written for Catholic parishes as a handy, how-to guide for their stewardship conversion efforts. *Stewardship: A Parish Handbook* is described as "an overview of the entire process of stewardship conversion" and "a practical reference manual that provides a one-stop resource for parish and diocesan leaders and involved laity who are engaged in developing and implementing local stewardship initiatives."

Every Catholic Christian has been exposed to the tenet that God is the source of all gifts and blessings. Intellectually, most Catholics acknowledge its validity. However, true stewardship conversion takes place only when we embrace this teaching with every emotional fiber of our being and begin to live the consequences it produces.

Once More With Feelings

"Feelings, nothing more than feelings…" is a musical phrase that has almost become a comic mantra for lounge lizards—those Frank Sinatra wannabes who seem to magically appear near every hotel piano bar. Feelings—emotions—are essential attributes of human nature. Let's explore how they relate to the topic of parish stewardship conversion.

According to one theory of social psychology, we humans are frequently buffeted between the left and right sides of our brains. The left side is the intellectual, analytical side; the right side is the intuitive, creative side. Based on observable behavioral characteristics, most people tend to be dominated by one side of the brain or the other.

Left-brainers tend to be logical, objective, structured, and controlled (that is, less emotional). They remember names, solve problems by breaking them into parts and moving sequentially to a solution, and prefer talking and writing ("*Tell* me how to do it"). Right-brainers are intuitive, subjective, fluid, and spontaneous (that is, more emotional). They remember faces, solve problems by looking at patterns and using hunches, and prefer drawing and manipulating objects ("*Show* me how to do it"). According to this viewpoint of human behavior, men and women should strive for total integration of both sides of their brains, much like a basketball player works to be equally facile with both hands.

Through the centuries, the Catholic Church has endured an uneasy relationship between its own left and right brain. It's evident that the Church values quasi-scientific, dispassionate philosophical and theological discourse; witness the accolades paid to the likes of Augustine, Thomas Aquinas, and Karl Rahner. But impassioned artistic expression has also been held in high regard; witness the massive historical collections of religious music, sculpture, paintings, and literature.

The latter notwithstanding, the institutional Church has always been suspicious of emotions. Expressions of feelings are portrayed as somehow less noble than intellectual pursuits, a sign of weakness, and perhaps even evidence of our sinful nature. (Dare we say it? Could this be one result of centuries of celibate male dominance within the Church?) Yet, in their 1992 pastoral, *Stewardship: A Disciple's Response*, the U.S. bishops challenged Catholics to convert to a stewardship way of life.

Conversion means a change of heart. Conversion is as much, if not more, emotional and attitudinal as it is logical and cognitive. In other words, stewardship conversion—whether its personal or parish—requires a synthesis of both left- and right-brain characteristics.

Stewardship conversion can take place only when individual Catholics and their parish communities recapture some of the same passionate Spirit that inflamed the hearts of the disciples on Pentecost. When the followers of Jesus burst from their hiding place on that magnificent day, they were not thinking dispassionately and logically; they were consumed with a desire to tell the world about the Jesus they loved so much. Who would deny that many of our parishes need a rekindling of the Pentecost fire? Programs such as Christ Renews His Parish and RENEW are proven catalysts for touching peoples' hearts and creating a climate for stewardship conversion.

We often use the word *spirit* to describe a great stirring of emotions. Consider, for example, how hard cheerleaders work to whip teams and fans into a frenzy at sporting events. Should the emotions associated with our faith be anything less than those we feel during a basketball or football game?

Am I Missing Something?

Everyone has benchmark life experiences, those momentous occurrences—sometimes negative, sometimes positive—that mark a significant milestone either in our personal growth or in our relationships with others. I had such an experience not long ago when my son gave me the best Christmas present I will ever receive. It was a piece of stone he had purchased at "Successories," a franchise store that can be found in many U.S. malls. On the stone was engraved the words "Attitude Is Everything."

I asked John why he had chosen this unusual gift. His response caught me completely off guard. He said, "Because I think that describes you, Dad." As I began to struggle with a lump in my throat, I posed another question, the one that produced my benchmark event. I asked: "But what do *you* think about that phrase?" He replied: "I think that's the key to all success in life."

I could not have scripted a better response; it was exactly what I hoped he would say. My heart leapt, and the lump in my throat swelled to painful proportions. At that moment I realized that my wife and I had achieved some level of success as parents and would not have to be excessively concerned about our son's personal and professional future.

Since you're reading these words, you're most likely a disciple of Jesus Christ. The definition of a disciple is "a follower, one who accepts and assists in spreading the doctrines of another." It's conceivable that a person can be a disciple without passion or emotion…just going through the motions and lifelessly performing obligatory tasks. Heaven knows we occasionally encounter teachers, coworkers, or service providers like that.

But there are several huge differences between followers of Jesus and generic disciples. In the first place, Christians have been baptized and confirmed. We have received the same Spirit that inspired the apostles on Pentecost; not as dramatically, of course—at least our hair was not in danger of being set on fire!

Christians have also been saved from the ravages of sin. We are the recipients of the results of Christ's magnificently selfless act of sacrifice *and subsequent resurrection* (note the emphasis—more about that later). Furthermore, we have been extraordinarily blessed by a loving and beneficent God who continuously showers us with blessings. God, the source of all, generously allows us the use of some of his "stuff" as we pass through our lifetimes.

With all of these splendid benefits associated with Christian discipleship, should we not be thrilled and bubbling over with joyful enthusiasm? Why, then, the seas of dead faces in many of our churches? Why the lackluster liturgies? Why the growing number of perpetually disgruntled spiritual leaders? Why the parishes where visitors and members alike feel unwelcome and unappreciated? Am I missing something here?

Church prayers and music are filled with words like joyful, celebrate, rejoice, happy, delight, and so on. Are we not called to be Easter people? Yet when one observes the demeanor of many of Christ's disciples, it's hard to experience the Good News of our salvation.

I have a recurring fantasy that Jesus decides to return for a midterm performance evaluation of the quality and character of discipleship in his church. After a quick look around for initial impressions, he says: "You know, folks, I really didn't intend for things to be this onerous or complicated!" He then reminds us of the job description he gave us as his followers: the two great commandments and the beatitudes. He reiterates the rewards that God has prepared for good and faithful stewards. He reminds us that he was fully human as well as divine when he walked the Jewish countryside. In fact, in spite of numerous artists' renderings of his suffering, he assures us that he has a sense of humor: He smiles when something pleases him; he laughs when something is funny. He concludes his brief visit with two quotes attributed to him by John the Evangelist: "In the world you face persecution. But take courage; I have conquered the world!" (16:33), and "I have said these things to you so that my joy may be in you, and that your joy may be complete" (15:11).

Finally, as he ascends once again into the clouds, we hear him exclaim: "Lighten up, folks! Remember: Attitude is everything!"

Two Little Words

Two words, when combined, may create the biggest impediment for Christians on their journey toward a total stewardship lifestyle: "I" (along with its grammatical cousins "me" and "my") and "stuff." Let's look at each word, then consider their potential impact on parish and individual stewardship conversion efforts when they are united.

The "I-me-my" trio probably comprises the most frequently used words in any language. Carrying on a conversation without the I-trio is nearly impossible. For self-absorbed people, the I-trio is an absolute addiction! Self-centeredness is, however, antithetical to Christian stewardship: the two cannot coexist in a faithful disciple of Jesus Christ. Best-selling author and leadership guru Ken Blanchard (*The One-Minute Manager*) believes that what he refers to as "EGO-addiction" is the biggest impediment to progress in any organization. He defines EGO as "Edging God Out" (more about this in a later reflection).

And what about "stuff?" George Carlin, at one time a comedian's comedian who, in recent years, has regrettably succumbed to the mistaken belief that antireligious vitriol and crude language are funny, once created a masterful routine about Americans' love affair with their "stuff." Here are a few of his observations: "Guys have stuff in their pockets, women have stuff in their purses. Your stuff is important so you gotta take care of it. You gotta have a place for your stuff. That's why you need a house—it's a place to keep your stuff. A house is a pile of stuff with a cover on it. You often leave your house to go get more stuff. That's what this country is all about: trying to get more stuff than anybody else. Eventually you get so much more stuff that you need a bigger house...."

Combining the "I-trio," "stuff," and "stewardship conversion" is much like dropping three pieces of dry ice into a container of water, then sealing it shut. The results are dangerously destructive. Self-centeredness, selfish ownership ("my stuff"), and Christian stewardship are simply incompatible. Why? Because disciples of Jesus Christ are compelled to recognize God as the source of all.

Here's what the U.S. bishops wrote in their 1992 pastoral letter: *Stewardship: A Disciple's Response*: "Disciples who practice stewardship recognize God as the origin of life, the giver of freedom, the source of all they have and are and will be....They know themselves to be recipients and caretakers of God's many gifts" (from the introduction).

We Christians profess to believe, among other things, that we own nothing. Sometimes, however, we get confused between civil law and God's law. On several occasions, Jesus tried to clarify this distinction for his followers. Yes, we may have deeds to our homes, titles for our cars, and receipts for various items of clothing, furnishings, and equipment in our "possession." But, in God's eyes, all of these things, including our lives, are just on loan. There's a simple proof for this. When we die, our accumulated stuff is inevitably transferred to others unless, of course, we manage to secure a cemetery plot large enough to take our possessions with us!

Listen to the bishops again: "This is a culture in which destructive 'isms'—materialism, relativism, hedonism, individualism, consumerism—exercise seductive, powerful influences....In some ways it may be harder to be a Christian steward today than at times in the past" (from the introduction).

Harder it may be. But, for disciples of Jesus, an option it is not.

An Impossible Exercise?

Here's a mental exercise that may be impossible for many Americans to perform. Try to imagine that you're a tribesman from a Third World country where your people are dying of starvation daily. One month ago you were suddenly transported to the United States and placed in the midst of a fairly typical middle-class family: mother, father, teenage son, and elementary-school daughter.

For the past thirty days, you have observed the family's lifestyle. You attended school with the children; you were with them as they spent time with their friends at malls, at fast-food restaurants, in their homes, or just cruisin'. You shadowed the parents at their workplaces, during their times of recreation, as they shopped, attended parties, and went to church. You listened to their conversations. You learned about their likes and dislikes, their concerns, the issues and difficulties they face, what makes them happy, what makes them sad, what makes them angry.

Now you have returned to your home neighborhood to report your experiences. Your friends and neighbors gather around to hear what it was like being with the North Americans. Since this exercise is pure fantasy, we can only imagine your thoughts and feelings as you relate some of the things you saw and overheard during your time with each family member:

- You watched the son buy a pair of sneakers for $150, and pay three times more for clothing items because they had certain names or symbols on them.
- At the daughter's elementary school, you saw the children throw away, in one month, enough food to feed your village for a year.
- You were with the mother as she spent hours selecting and applying just the right makeup for each occasion, and shopped for clothes—even though her closets were overflowing—because, "I don't have a thing to wear!"
- You accompanied the father as he negotiated a $400-per-month lease payment on a luxury car he couldn't afford to

buy outright, and watched as he dropped a $5 bill in the collection basket at Mass each Sunday.

- You overheard numerous conversations about how important it was for this family to live in the "right" neighborhood, drive the "right" kind of car, attend the "right" schools, wear the "right" clothes, and socialize with the "right" people.

As you recount your experiences, your neighbors stare at you in wide-eyed wonder. To them, your report sounds like a combination of science fiction and fairy tales. When you finish, your neighbors sit in stunned silence for a few minutes. Then, one by one, they arise, and, mumbling and shaking their heads, they slowly return to the task of looking for the means to feed themselves and their family members for just one more day.

At this point, we who are called to be good stewards of God's many gifts might recall a few words from the New Testament:

"For where your treasure is, there your heart will be also" (Matthew 6:21).

"You cannot serve both God and wealth" (Matthew 6:24).

"The measure you give will be the measure you get back" (Luke 6:38).

"From everyone to whom much has been given, much will be required" (Luke 12:48).

"In all this I have given you an example that by such work we must support the weak, remembering the words of the Lord Jesus, for he himself said, 'It is more blessed to give than to receive'" (Acts 20:35).

"So then, each of us will be accountable to God" (Romans 14:12).

O Happy Sacrifice

For many Catholics who were educated in the faith prior to Vatican II, the word *sacrifice* is forever linked to Christ's death. This association was aggressively nurtured in Catholic schools through realistic representations of a bloody, bruised Jesus on the way to Calvary and ultimately nailed to the cross. Many older Catholics recall Father or Sister reading to them from a book entitled *A Doctor at Calvary* by Pierre Barbet—a graphic description of the excruciating sufferings of Jesus during his final hours. (Director Mel Gibson's movie *The Passion of the Christ* is a stunning visual representation of Barbet's prose.) Therefore, it's understandable that, in addition to Christ's death, many Catholics may associate the concept of sacrifice with physical and/or emotional pain. But is this perception accurate?

One dictionary defines *sacrifice* as "the destruction or surrender of something for the sake of something else"; another defines it as "the forfeiture of one thing for another thing considered to be of greater value." Giving up one thing for another could indeed trigger a difficult change or produce a distressing sense of loss, but not necessarily. "Sacrifice" and "suffering" are not synonyms; neither is there an essential causal relationship between the two; nor are the two inescapably connected. People gladly and willingly sacrifice when they stop smoking to save their lives and the lives of those around them, or when they diet and exercise to improve their physical and emotional health, or when they save money to buy something they've always wanted.

We raise this issue because some stewardship advocates are fond of the phrase "sacrificial giving," which is sometimes described as "giving until it hurts." If sharing time, talent, and treasure induces pain and suffering, who can ever become the "cheerful giver" (2 Corinthians 9:7) whom God loves? Indeed, how can we reconcile good stewardship with this quote from the Acts of the Apostles: "We must support the weak, remembering the words of the Lord Jesus, for he himself said, 'It is more blessed to give than to receive'" (20:35).

Perhaps the confusion lies in a fundamental misunderstanding of the relationship between sacrifice and that portion of our time, talent, and treasure that we choose to share with others. In the first place, as we've mentioned several times above, our time, talent, and treasure are really not ours. They're actually God's property temporarily on loan to us. If my giving is based on gratitude to God, who is the source of all that I am and have, it's easy to be a cheerful giver. As one deeply committed steward once observed: "When I share time, talent, and treasure with others, I feel liberated and invigorated, not depressed or put upon. To me, it's another opportunity to thank God for being so good to me, and it makes me even more conscious of the many blessings I have received."

For good stewards, sacrificial giving should not be "giving until it hurts," but "giving until it feels good." The good steward's motto is found in Psalm 116:

> What shall I return to the LORD
> for all his bounty to me?

STEP 2

Commitment
of Leadership

The personal commitment of the bishop or pastor is absolutely necessary for the success of diocesan and parish stewardship and development efforts. In addition, wherever possible, parishes and dioceses should have active stewardship committees whose members include a representative group of pastoral and lay leaders willing to pray, discuss, learn, and lead.

The leadership team commissioned by the bishop or pastor should be responsible for (1) stewardship formation and educational programs in the diocese or parish, and (2) oversight of the parish's or diocese's efforts to promote gifts of time, talent, and treasure for annual capital, and endowment purposes. Professional staff and/or consultants should be employed where appropriate and where diocesan or parish resources permit. As in all aspects of church life, the collaborative leadership and active involvement of many people are essential to the success of parish and diocesan stewardship efforts.

STEWARDSHIP: A DISCIPLE'S RESPONSE (PAGE 59)

The New Leadership Imperative

Several years ago, the young associate pastor of a parish in a small midwestern town was chatting with the elderly founder of the community's largest and most successful business. This industrial pioneer was renowned for his hands-on leadership style. He was often seen sweeping the front steps of his company's corporate headquarters! At the time, in his seventies and nearing retirement, he delighted in recounting how he started his company and built it into a major regional economic force.

But he was also concerned about his legacy. He remarked that "today's young people just don't seem to have the same drive and passion that my generation did, nor do they have the same dedication to quality work or devotion to customer service." The young priest quickly realized that this businessman wasn't talking about young children or adolescents. He was referring to his own children who, at the time, were in their forties and fifties!

On another occasion, a diocesan development director was visiting with a captain of industry who had followed a dream that eventually became a Fortune 500 company. The development director asked the distinguished octogenarian what was the key to his success. He replied: "When I started my company, I knew I didn't know everything I needed to know. So I surrounded myself with people who were smarter than me. I still do that, and I'm careful to reward people well for everything they do for me and our company." These stories highlight several attributes of skillful, competent leadership.

More than ever, the U.S. Catholic Church needs skillful, competent leaders who are not only well versed in religious and spiritual matters, but are also in tune with current social and cultural realities. Prior to the Second Vatican Council, the flow chart for Church authority and decision-making resembled a pyramid, with God at the top, followed by the pope, cardinals, bishops, priests, religious, and the laity forming the base. Vatican II produced an organizational model that looks like a circle, with Jesus Christ at the center, surrounded by all of the entities found in the earlier pyramid model as well as a huge ecumenical component.

The consequences of this massive shift in the style and substance of

Church organizational structures continue to unfold daily. For example, the days are gone when bishops and priests were among only a few highly educated people in their communities. In every parish and diocese, lay-men and women with highly developed skills and talents are waiting to be called forth by competent Church leaders. Given this new environment, parish and diocesan stewardship conversion will happen only when laypeople become engaged in the process and are encouraged in their stewardship pursuits by pastoral leaders.

Autocratic governance and benevolent dictatorships are obsolete. Today's Church leaders must be skilled in building consensus, processing discernment, and facilitating collaboration. They must understand such concepts as value-added service, total quality management, and the principle of subsidiarity, to name just a few. Furthermore, numerous personnel and human relation issues that were completely unknown in the first two-thirds of the twentieth century have become major driving forces in the Church workplace, just as they have in the business community.

So what's a poor, struggling Church leader to do? In the words of that master of obfuscation, Yogi Berra: "You can observe a lot by watching." Parish and diocesan leaders can learn much by studying today's successful business models. In recent years, disciples of post-World War II socio-industrial pioneers, such as W. Edwards Deming, have created extraordinarily effective leadership styles and management strategies that have many worthwhile applications for Church environments.

The "Business" and "Management" sections of bookstores and libraries are heavily stocked with books containing marvelous insights and practical suggestions for Church leaders struggling with their new roles as fiscal managers and human relations practitioners. Each decade tends to produce its own popular series of leadership and management philosophies. In the 1980s, Japanese management techniques and re-engineering were quite the rage. Two recent bestsellers with strong messages for today's Church leaders are *Jesus CEO* by Laurie Beth Jones, and Stephen R. Covey's *The Seven Habits of Highly Effective People*. Each of these books would be an excellent resource for parish and diocesan staff leadership retreats.

In the midst of shifting paradigms of Church leadership, there is one particularly troubling concern that was uncovered several years ago in a landmark study funded by Lilly Endowment. Researchers designed instruments to ascertain the availability and quality of mainline Catholic and Protestant seminary programs devoted to skill development in the areas of leadership, management, and stewardship, and to measure pastors' attitudes and perceptions about these three topics. The results—published in 1992 under the title *The Reluctant Steward*—disclosed a major contradiction: "...mainline Protestant and Catholic pastors who were surveyed strongly agree that administration and finance are their greatest areas of frustration. At the same time, while they believe that seminaries should do more to prepare those who will come after them for administrative and financial leadership, they do not express any strong interest in continuing education courses or workshops that might help them to be better stewards of their congregations' human, physical, and financial resources."

Not only were the surveyed pastors generally unwilling to improve their administrative and interpersonal leadership skills, the researchers found much ambivalence among seminary leaders regarding their responsibility to provide courses in the areas of leadership, stewardship, and management. Even when such courses are available, they are rarely part of the required curriculum. A follow-up to the Lilly study, published in 2002 as *The Reluctant Steward Revisited*, found that nothing had changed in the intervening decade.

These findings indicate a "status quo" mentality that is unsuitable for today's Church. Motivational pundits tell us: "Success is a journey, not a destination"; "The person on the top of the mountain didn't fall there"; and "Whether you think you can, or whether you think you can't, you are right."

The latter maxim contains a kernel of hope, despite the discouraging results of the Lilly Endowment study. We now know that the sage was wrong: old dogs *can* learn new tricks. Older Americans are staying in the workforce in record numbers and they're choosing to go back to school to be retrained to meet today's job demands. Partly because of this burgeoning lifetime-learning phenomenon, educators are finally realizing that "learning how to learn" is a critically important life skill they must develop in their young students. People who love to learn never become stagnant and rarely experience burnout. They relish new challenges, constantly seeking another mountain to climb, another obstacle to overcome, or another skill to acquire.

Parish and diocesan leaders must grasp something our brothers and sisters in the business community know all too well: inertia is unacceptable. At the same time U.S. Catholics are trying to assimilate stewardship into their lives, Church leaders are being challenged to adopt new leadership styles that are required to facilitate the stewardship conversion process.

The leadership ideal for every Christian disciple is—or should be—Jesus Christ, the Magnificent Steward. Our friends in the business world can teach us many things about the traits and qualities that made Jesus such a dynamic, influential leader. A good steward is open to the movement of the Spirit from every possible source.

Pastoral Leadership and Stewardship

A senior executive of a Fortune 500 company, who had opted to take an early retirement package rather than be transferred to a city far from his children and grandchildren, recently accepted his bishop's offer to supervise the administration of diocesan services and programs. He was thrilled by the prospect of working for an organization whose corporate ethic was based on altruistic gospel values and Christian respect rather than bottom-line, profit-oriented business motives. However, within a short time, he was somewhat surprised to find that the Catholic Church is truly the people of God, with the accent on "people," that is, imperfect, flawed human beings.

One of his lay coworkers, who also had worked in the for-profit sector before accepting a diocesan position, noticed his colleague's growing dismay and offered this analogy: "For the average Catholic, the prospect of working for the Church is very much like being a passenger on a cruise ship," said the coworker. "For the vacationers, everything about a cruise appears glamorous: accommodations, food, amenities, scenery, and so on. But if you go into the engine room, you're likely to find some unpleasant things like heat, dirt, and excessive noise; it's not a particularly appealing place."

"My friend," the coworker continued, "you are now in the Church's engine room. Things may not always be so nice. You will increasingly find that the Church is a community of Christ's disciples who are also Adam's and Eve's progeny: fallible human beings with biases and prejudices, strengths and weaknesses, skills and talents, and lots of personal emotional baggage. In other words, human beings are human beings, no matter what career choices they have made."

No sooner had the new diocesan employee begun to adjust to the human nature of Christ's Church, when he was confronted with a second important insight: in spite of the growing priest shortage, or perhaps because of it, pastors are still an extremely influential power group within the Catholic Church. By their attitudes and support—or absence of them—pastors can make or break any parish project or diocesan program. And they do this with impunity because there is little, if any, systematic accountability attached to their role. This was a particularly difficult reality for the new diocesan employee to accept because he had spent so many years in a typical for-profit milieu that valued teamwork, expected compliance, and required productivity—or else! So what does all of this have to do with stewardship? The answer is: everything. Individual stewardship conversion begins to happen when sinful Christians acknowledge their dependence on God, who is the source of all grace and blessings. Parish stewardship conversion requires strong, positive, supportive pastoral leadership. In so many ways, pastors and pastoral administrators—imperfect humans like their parishioners—hold the key to successful stewardship conversion.

In 1987, the U.S. Bishops' Committee on Priestly Life and Ministry of the National Conference of Catholic Bishops published a landmark document entitled *A Shepherd's Care: Reflections on the Changing Role of Pastor*. The primary audience for this document was "pastors themselves and those who will be pastors someday." As with any official Church publication, it's impossible to know how many pastors or pastors-to-be actually read and absorbed *A Shepherd's Care* at the time it was published or since. However, because of rapidly changing pastoral leadership models in the U.S. Church, the observations and projections contained in *A Shepherd's Care* are even more relevant today.

The authors of *A Shepherd's Care,* speaking for the U.S. bishops, masterfully and candidly reviewed how the pastor's roles (leadership, teaching, and pastoral care), relationships (with bishops, parishioners, and fellow priests, deacons, and lay ministers), and environment (in the parish, diocese, and universal Church) have been evolving since the Second Vatican Council—and not without pain and difficulties. We are beginning to see, for example, that the shortage of priests in many dioceses can have a direct, often negative impact on the stewardship conversion efforts of some parishes. This is happening with increased frequency as bishops fill pastoral vacancies with any available priest.

Here's what the U.S. bishops said about this practice in 1987: "Not all priests have the ability or the desire to exercise pastoral leadership as pastor.…Becoming a pastor should not be automatic or be an assumed 'promotion.' It certainly should not be simply viewed as a reward for years of service.…The pastorate is a ministry that must be learned and mastered.…Focused theological training, collaborative skills and techniques, and fundamental principles of organization and administration are only some of the requirements for effective pastoring" (page 15).

Parish stewardship conversion will not happen without the ardent, competent support of pastors or pastoral administrators and their staff members. Parish servant leaders must be sincerely committed to stewardship and model it in their own lives. This means providing the kind of collaborative, compassionate leadership needed to create a parish community that is rooted in prayer—particularly the celebration of the Eucharist—and that is characterized by a welcoming spirit and outstanding service for God's people. The stewardship way of life must be woven into the fabric of parish life.

A Shepherd's Care is a truly prophetic document that deserves another serious look by bishops, pastors, and pastors-in-waiting who are currently charting the course for the U.S. Catholic Church during these early years of a new millennium. Furthermore, if it is not already, *A Shepherd's Care* should be required reading in every seminary pastoral preparation program. The engine room of the Catholic Church does not have to be a forbidding environment.

You Might Be a Stewardship Leader If...

At times, everyone is called to be a leader. Parish stewardship conversion is a process that requires visionary pastoral leadership on several different levels: pastor, staff members, parish council, finance committee, and other key volunteers. Leadership is a somewhat enigmatic commodity. Most of us recognize it in others, but we're sometimes unsure about when it applies to us. Here's a checklist of items to help you assess your leadership acumen.

You might be a stewardship leader if...

You understand why Jesus was such an influential person.

You're a good listener.

You have the ability, when necessary, to move people to willing action.

You know the difference between managers and leaders, and when a situation calls for one or the other.

You have a working knowledge of the elements of servant leadership.

You have a clear vision of what you want to accomplish and know how to get others excited about it.

You expect excellence from yourself and others.

You can identify talents and abilities in others and you're able to delegate responsibilities which match them.

You're skilled at giving people the tools they need to get the job done.

You're not afraid of feedback and evaluation; in fact, you actively seek them as opportunities for growth and improvement.

You can be a coach or a cheerleader on demand.

You enjoy your work and you're able to transmit your enjoyment to others.

You have a realistic grasp of your own strengths and weaknesses.

You are in control of your time.

You recognize when change is in order and you're flexible enough to embrace it.

You take good care of your physical, mental, social and spiritual health, and you encourage people you work with to do the same.

You are committed to lifelong learning.

You have a sense of humor, especially about yourself.

Humility and integrity are not just words in a dictionary; they can legitimately be used to describe you.

You have a positive attitude, no matter what you encounter.

When you reach an impasse or encounter a major hurdle, one of your first thoughts is: *What would Jesus do?*

A Patron Saint for (Church?) Leaders

If the world's leading industrialists were asked to nominate three candidates from whom one would be selected as their honorary "patron saint," the name "W. Edwards Deming" would undoubtedly appear on most lists. William Edwards Deming was born in Iowa in 1900. In 1907, his family moved to a forty-acre plot of land in Wyoming where they lived a life of poverty and hardship. Deming's biographers credit his harsh frontier upbringing for shaping his personal style and exemplary values that included caring for people you're responsible for, cooperation is important, waste is deadly, and always strive for the best in everything you do. Deming was not a religious leader, but what bishop, priest, religious, or layperson would not want to emulate these qualities in a leadership role?

Deming concluded his formal education with a doctorate in math from Yale University in 1928. Following that he became a researcher for the U.S. Department of Agriculture. There he developed a precise statistical style that he later applied to industrial production and management. His growing reputation as a creative industrial consultant earned him an invitation in the 1950s to come to Japan to help that country rebuild its economy and industrial base following World War II. While in Japan, he developed and taught the Japanese his now-famous *Fourteen-Point Program to Improve Quality and Productivity.* His program started an industrial revolution that quickly turned Japan into a major economic world power. Eventually, U.S. business leaders realized the value of Deming's ideas and began to adopt them in this country.

When a parish or a diocese commits to promoting a total stewardship way of life, it also commits itself to excellence in pastoral ministry. Deming's message has profound implications for people who are striving for excellence in any organizational endeavor, including stewardship conversion. With a little creative imagination, Deming's fourteen points can be favorably translated into "Church" language and help parishes and dioceses focus their energies and resources on pastoral excellence.

Here's a five-point sample of Deming's brilliant directives, translated for Church leaders:

- *Create constancy of purpose toward improvement of product and service.*
  Translation: Parish and diocesan leaders should formulate and promote a stewardship-based vision of pastoral excellence for the communities they serve. Then, in cooperation with all of the faithful, develop a plan to move relentlessly toward that vision. Would Jesus expect anything less from his disciples?

- *Adopt the new philosophy*
  Translation: The basic tenets of the Catholic faith are immutable, but the accidentals that surround them are in a constant state of flux. The Church must learn to adapt more quickly. The competition for souls is fierce. A clever wordsmith once observed: "Even if you're on the right track, you'll get run over if you just stand there."

- *Improve constantly and forever the system of production and service*
  Translation: Two questions should drive each day's activities in a diocese or parish: (1) "How can we be better disciples of Jesus Christ today?" and (2) "How can we do better as a community of Christ's disciples tomorrow?"

- *Drive out fear, so that everyone may work effectively for the company*
  Translation: No member of a Christian community should ever be reluctant to approach pastoral leaders with an idea, a problem, or a concern. Our discipleship in Jesus Christ is our common bond. Living as good stewards is our common goal.

- *Break down barriers between departments*
  Translation: Interparochial cooperation, collaboration, and collegial leadership must replace narrow-minded parochialism as one step toward weathering the clergy shortage crisis facing so many U.S. dioceses today.

A full treatment of Deming's wisdom can be found in the 1998 edition of his landmark book, *Out of the Crisis*, originally published in 1982 by MIT, Cambridge, Massachusetts. It's fascinating reading. Just ask the business leaders in your parish!

Ego Addiction

"There are two types of people: those who come into a room and say, 'Well, here I am,' and those who come in and say, 'Ah, there you are.'"

FREDERICK L. COLLINS

Ken Blanchard is probably best known for his popular book *The One-Minute Manager*. Unfortunately, this book doesn't do justice to Blanchard's full range of talents either as a prolific writer or as a highly sought-after business consultant. Included in Blanchard's impressive bibliography are books coauthored with such personalities as Rev. Norman Vincent Peale, the godfather of "positive thinking"; Don Shula, former coach of the Miami Dolphins; Bill Hybels, pastor of the country's premier megachurch, Willow Creek Community Church; and Laurie Beth Jones, author of *Jesus CEO*.

During a seminar sponsored by the Indianapolis-based Greenleaf Center for Servant Leadership, Blanchard offered a particularly salient insight that has enormous significance for any diocese or parish considering or already engaged in a process of stewardship conversion. It's an insight that is also profoundly relevant to the U.S. Catholic Church following the dark days of multiple disclosures about the human frailties of a few of those who were ordained to be spiritual leaders.

Here's what Blanchard said: "There is no more destructive addiction in any organization than ego addiction." He went on to clarify that ego addiction to him means "Edging God Out." From his perspective, ego addiction is the antithesis of true servant leadership, a concept that was first created by Robert K. Greenleaf in 1970 with a small essay entitled "The Servant as Leader." In Greenleaf's mind, leaders tend to fall into one of two categories: servant-first and leader-first. Greenleaf was convinced that the greatest leaders are servant-first, that is, the kind of leaders who make sure that other people's highest priority needs are being served.

What is servant leadership? Greenleaf describes it this way: "The best test (of servant leadership) is: Do those served grow as persons? Do they, while being served, become healthier, wiser, freer, more autonomous, more likely themselves to become servants? And, what is the effect on the least privileged in society; will they benefit, or, at least, not be further deprived?" Could any style of leadership be more Christlike?

Blanchard's ego-addicted leaders are Greenleaf's "leader-first" leaders. Their personal needs and well-being are their primary concern, not the needs and well-being of the individuals or organizations which they serve. They tend to be controlling, critical, manipulative, mistrustful, and close-minded. They are often obsessed with "being right" or "having all the answers." In the extreme, they are either blustering "my-way-or-the-highway" bullies or diffident, passive-aggressive scoundrels.

When a diocese or parish chooses to embark on a stewardship

conversion voyage, virtually every element of its operation becomes subject to review. Inevitably, some things will have to change. If the leaders of that diocese or parish suffer from Blanchard's ego addiction, the voyage will most certainly end well short of its destination.

Bless Me, Employees...
Sins of (Church) Bosses

Here are five leadership sins often committed by bosses. When Church leaders are the guilty persons, these transgressions can have a profoundly negative effect on diocesan or parish efforts to achieve total stewardship conversion.

1. "I show my employees how much they are appreciated by paying them well."

   When employees were asked to identify and rank order the things they wanted most in their jobs, the top three items were

   † full appreciation of work done
   † feeling of "being in on things"
   † help with personal problems

   When bosses were asked what they thought their employees wanted, the top three responses were:

   † high wages
   † job security
   † promotion in the company

There are two powerful messages here: a paycheck is *not* a primary motivator—it simply keeps employees from quitting—and bosses who do not regularly express appreciation, share decision-making, and show empathy for employees' concerns *might* get what they pay for—but not much more.

2. "Why don't my people know about (fill in any event or issue here)? After all, I sent them a memo!"

Let's review a few facts: our mailboxes (including e-mail) overflow with junk mail; we're bombarded with information from multiple media sources every waking minute; as a society, we're moving and switching jobs at a record pace. Will a single, bulk-mailed, form letter to parishioners sufficiently communicate important information? Not a chance!

When it comes to communicating with parishioners, remember that you're competing with high-powered advertising professionals who are skilled at capturing people's "TOMA" (Top of Mind Awareness). We can learn from them. Effective communication these days requires multiple media and repetition. Parish activities and other important information should be publicized several times for several weeks in several ways: pulpit announcements, articles in bulletins and newsletters, well-placed flyers, direct mail, and, when appropriate, items in local newspapers as well as TV and radio public service announcements.

3. "You want to do what?! Absolutely not!"

Does this sound familiar? You give your boss a great idea to improve service, or to generate more income, or to increase employee morale, and the first response is always: "No." Not "Maybe," not "Let's consider it"—just a pure and simple "No." After a steady diet of these idea-killing, "knee-jerk" no responses, an employee would need superhuman self-determination to continue to approach the boss (read "bishop" or "pastor") with more good ideas or suggestions!

4. "They're really good workers, but…"

Here's a surefire clue you're dealing with problem employees: you say something complimentary about them, yet feel immediately compelled to add a phrase beginning with "but." "He does good work, *but* he's so temperamental." "She's very efficient, *but* she's always late for work." "He's very talented, *but* he's absent a lot on Mondays and Fridays." The boss's sin is not to address such issues quickly and decisively because problem employees invariably affect the performance and morale of fellow workers and volunteers.

5. "Is it the boss's idea yet?"

This sin is a spinoff of number 3 above. An employee's hot idea that received a cool reception from the boss weeks ago suddenly reemerges when the boss announces that he or she has just come up with a great innovation! Dime-store psychologists might speculate that such bosses are subconsciously fearful that a subordinate might expose their shortcomings and claim their jobs. Great leaders acknowledge their inadequacies and surround themselves with people who compensate for them.

STEP 3

Hospitality, Evangelization, and Outreach

Communities known for the vitality of their faith and for the quality of their service to people in need invariably inspire others to participate in their ministries and to be generous in their financial support. With this in mind, parishes and dioceses that seek to promote gifts of time, talent, and treasure to support the mission and ministries of the Church should first demonstrate that they are welcoming communities with a commitment to preaching the Gospel and serving the needs of others.

Parishes and dioceses should not make commitments to hospitality, evangelization, and outreach simply because this will enhance their ability to recruit volunteers or raise money. These activities should be the natural outgrowth of a parish's or diocese's mission. However, dioceses and parishes that seek to increase participation or to raise additional funds would do well to look to the effectiveness of their efforts to welcome, evangelize, and serve.

As an integral part of their commitment to stewardship as a way of life, parish and diocesan leaders should initiate and implement stewardship projects unrelated to the Church itself,

for example, conservation of natural resources, environmental im-
provements, advocacy projects to benefit the poor and needy and
affirming family values. In addition, as a witness to the value of
generous giving that is not based on obligation or need, dioceses
and parishes should try to make donations of time, talent, and trea-
sure to people and causes (in their local communities and through-
out the world) that are over and above their participation in as-
sessments and second collections.

Stewardship: A Disciple's Response (page 60)

Hello, Do You Come Here Often?
The Welcoming Parish

Is your parish a welcoming, hospitable community? Pose this question
to active members of any Catholic parish in the United States and chances
are the answer will be an emphatic "yes." So why is it that many Catholics report that when they attend Mass in their own parishes, or as visitors to other parishes, they feel just as much like a stranger when they
leave the church as when they entered? Perhaps it's because we often
confuse fellowship (that is, socializing with relatives, friends, and ac-
quaintances) with hospitality. Just because a parish mission statement
or a banner hanging on a wall proclaims "We're a Welcoming Parish," it
doesn't make it so!

All of us have experienced hospitality (and the absence of it) in restaurants, stores, and homes. Pleasant sights, sounds, smells, and human
behavior converge to create a welcoming atmosphere. Hospitable is defined as "given to generous and cordial reception of guests" and "offer-
ing a pleasant or sustaining environment." In other words, hospitality is
as much ambience as it is activity.

One of the hallmarks of a total stewardship parish is its hospitality.
Parishes that are renowned for having achieved a communal stewardship way of life have a welcoming spirit that is immediately obvious to
anyone who enters their confines.

So, is your parish a welcoming, hospitable community? How do you know? Is it because you're accosted by someone with a "Greeter" name tag who shoves a hymnal in your hand as you enter church? Is it because your parish occasionally offers coffee and doughnut fellowship after Mass? Is it because, for years, you meet with the same group of friends to quilt, or work the bingo, or prepare the monthly parish dinner, and a new member hasn't joined your group since the great flood?

Or is it, rather, because you will find the pastor and parish staff members "working the crowd" at every parish gathering? Is it because great efforts are made to seek out and welcome visitors and strangers at every Mass or parish event? Is it because newcomers to the parish are formally and publicly introduced to the rest of the members, and are quickly drawn into active parish participation? Is it because parish leaders frequently acknowledge and express their gratitude for the time and talent that parishioners share? Is it because parishioners feel they are well-served? Is it because front-line staff members or volunteers are always pleasant, courteous, and solicitous? Is it because every parishioner shares equally in the responsibility to create a welcoming, hospitable environment?

We should note one major obstacle to parish hospitality caused by a common Catholic practice. This true story illustrates the issue: A Catholic priest and a Protestant minister were sharing some of the challenges currently facing their respective flocks. The minister mentioned that his congregation was growing so rapidly that he had to build a larger church. The priest said: "Why don't you just add another service on the weekend?" The minister stared at his friend incredulously for a moment, then responded: "That would destroy my congregation! We gather as one faith family each week for worship and fellowship. If I add another service, it would irreparably divide my people. A larger church is my only option!"

The minister's solution may, of course, be unrealistic for many Catholic parishes. But we know from experience that most practicing Catholics attend the same Mass each week. As a result, they become acquainted with only a portion of the total parish membership. Unless a parish has several opportunities for all of its members to socialize, it's difficult for parishioners to distinguish fellow members from strangers.

A stewardship parish should conduct an annual evaluation of its hospitality milieu. Several groups should be considered when a parish asks itself, "How welcoming are we?"

Do we open our doors to current members (with two subgroups: the involved and the uninvolved), guests and visitors, seekers, C&E (Christmas and Easter) attenders, newcomers, catechumens in the RCIA program, and the "unaware," that is, anyone not found in the other groups who is therefore a candidate for evangelization?

How does the parish make all of these groups feel welcome? Who is responsible for monitoring hospitality activities? What systems are in place to elicit feedback about the efficacy of these activities?

A welcoming spirit is infectious, much like when you graciously hold a door for someone, or let another vehicle go ahead of you in traffic (you know—the kinds of things we tend to do during the Christmas season but not the rest of the year!), and you notice that the person you helped extends the same courtesy to the next person in line. Hospitality is as contagious as a smile or yawn, and it can significantly affect every aspect of parish life in a positive, uplifting way.

In truth, there's no such thing as a "welcoming, hospitable parish." There are only welcoming, hospitable parish leaders and parishioners whose collective efforts produce a welcoming, hospitable atmosphere. So, once again, we pose the question: **Is your parish a truly hospitable community? Really?**

Sunday Shoes

There's one characteristic—among others—that sets great teachers apart from average teachers. Great teachers, including religious educators, seem to be on an obsessive quest, continually looking for more and better ways to motivate and excite their students. With this in mind, consider the following anecdote a parish catechist related about an experience she had during a recent Christmas holiday season.

Facing the relentless commercial Christmas juggernaut, the catechist conceived an activity that she thought would engage her primary-grade students in the true spirit of the season. She suggested that each of them pick one of their unopened Christmas presents and give it to a needy child. When her students told their parents about her proposition, several mothers called her to voice their displeasure. Each in her own way, the mothers said, "What if the children choose to give away one of their most expensive gifts? We would be very unhappy if that happened!"

What's the stewardship message here? What do you imagine Jesus would say to these parents? Perhaps this next story will provide a clue:

An eighty-six-year-old member of a parish stewardship committee once stunned her fellow committee members by admitting that she occasionally attended a nearby nondenominational, evangelical "megachurch." "Don't get we wrong," she said. "I love the Catholic Church and my parish and I still go to Mass here on the weekends when I attend the other church. I just enjoy some of the things they do there."

When asked to be more specific, she recounted this powerful, moving incident from one of her visits to the "other church." On that Sunday morning, the preacher spoke with great emotion about an impoverished Christian community in a Third World country his congregation had "adopted" and that he and a few members of his congregation had recently visited. Most pressing, he said, was the need for good shoes. Almost all of the members of their adopted congregation had to go barefoot, which in that country's subtropical heat was often quite painful. He concluded his impassioned remarks by asking the congregation to donate their shoes for the people of their adopted community. But here's the rub: He knew that his people were thinking: "That's a good idea. When we get home, we'll go through our closets, dig out all our old, worn, smelly shoes, and bring them to church next week so they can be sent to those poor people." Reading their thoughts, the preacher said: "Folks, what would Jesus do in a case like this? Would he not want to honor the poor people of our adopted congregation by giving them his best, not his cast offs? After all, didn't he give us his best by sacrificing his very life? So I'm asking you to follow his example and give them your best. I'm asking you to remove the shoes you're now wearing—your 'Sunday best'—and donate them to our adopted brothers and sisters."

What happened next moved the entire congregation to tears of joy: every man, woman, and child in that church on that Sunday morning removed their shoes and, when the service ended, went home in their stockinged or bare feet! Later, hundreds of pairs of good shoes were boxed up and mailed to the adopted congregation.

What's the stewardship message here?

We are the stewards of God's many gifts and blessings. Jesus Christ is the Magnificent Steward. He most certainly gave his best for us. Can we be his disciples and do anything less?

Little Bo Peep Was Wrong!

The pastor of an extraordinarily successful stewardship parish was once asked what factors contributed to his parish's remarkable commitment to a stewardship way of life. In the midst of his response, he mentioned that, in his early years as pastor, he became quite distressed whenever one of his parishioners left his parish and joined another nearby parish. Finally, after years of fretting and lost sleep, he decided that he would personally visit any members of his flock who switched parishes and conduct his own "exit interview" to find out what prompted their decision. This practice, although at times painful and humiliating, has helped him identify and correct counterproductive practices and destructive attitudes in his parish.

This pastor is apparently the type of shepherd about whom Jesus spoke, who will "leave the ninety-nine [sheep] on the mountains and go in search of the one that went astray?" (Matthew 18:12). In other words, Ms. Peep—you can't just "leave them alone and they'll come home"— you must go after them and entice them to return to the fold. A related business principle states: "It costs five to ten times as much to find new customers than to keep the ones you already have."

We've mentioned elsewhere in this book that people who live and work in the nonprofit world can learn much from the business community about such things as public relations, marketing, and accountability; likewise, those who labor in the for-profit world can learn much from the nonprofit community about values, justice, and ethical behavior. With this in mind, let's explore the implications of the business maxim quoted above when applied to a parish or diocese engaged in a process of stewardship conversion.

To understand these implications, we first must review a popular business construct known as Customer Relationship Management

(CRM). CRM is a bit difficult to define because it encompasses a wide range of issues and techniques that are often unique to an organization that practices it. At its core, however, CRM is a customer-centric business philosophy that involves developing strategies designed to create a close relationship with each customer. The goal of CRM is to establish and maintain customer loyalty.

The best Customer Relationship Management practitioners are master students of the human condition. An organization committed to CRM seeks to learn as much as it can about its customers and prospective customers so that it can produce and promote products and services that truly make a connection with them. The message that an organization seeks to convey to its customers through CRM is quite simple: we know not only who you are but also what makes you tick: how you think, what drives your decision-making, and what we must do to keep you returning to us time and again.

In a Catholic parish, parishioners are the primary customers; it's they who support the parish and expect services from the parish in return. Parishioner loyalty depends in large measure on how well the parish works its own brand of CRM that, in Church parlance, falls largely under the heading of evangelization. Christian evangelization is the business of bringing Christ's Good News to all of humanity. One goal of a parish's evangelization activities is to create within each parishioner a sense of ownership of, and accountability for, the entire parish family. In a Catholic stewardship parish, the CRM bar should be raised to the highest level.

From a parish perspective, evangelization encompasses a wide array of activities and tactics directed toward three broad categories of people: the unchurched and "seekers," current parishioners, and lapsed Catholics. In CRM language, evangelization which targets the first category requires certain marketing skills and strategies geared toward customer acquisition. Evangelization directed toward current members (category two) requires techniques designed to promote and solidify customer (parishioner) loyalty.

One of the most difficult challenges for a stewardship parish is what to do about lapsed Catholics. It's no secret that Catholics in many parts of the U.S. are leaving the Church in ever-increasing numbers. It's a phenomenon that touches practically every Catholic family. In one Midwestern diocese, for example, a ten-year study recently completed by the diocesan office of stewardship and development showed that weekend Mass attendance has been on a steady decline in fifty of the seventy parishes. In fact, since 1994, overall diocesan Mass attendance has dropped 10 percent. In addition, many pastors reported that a substantial number of new members who entered the Church each year through RCIA programs seemed to disappear after a few months.

When these facts were presented at a parish stewardship committee meeting, one member remarked: "But our church is nearly full at all weekend Masses!" to which another member replied: "I have just two words for you: Christmas and Easter. Have you not noticed something different at our Masses on those two holidays? The church is bursting at the seams! We obviously have an evangelization problem."

Efforts to address this problem fall under the heading of a specialized aspect of Christian evangelization commonly called "reconciliation." Reconciliation, in a parish setting, refers to any attempt to draw marginal or lapsed parishioners into full participation in parish life.

Reconciliation touches several tiers within a parish community, such as members who attend regularly but are not actively engaged, borderline members (Christmas and Easter Catholics), members who leave the parish when they discover a more favorable nearby Catholic parish, "seeker" members who find a more suitable spiritual home in a local non-Catholic church, and members who abandon religion completely. When taken as a whole, most U.S. Catholics probably fall into one of these five categories.

What can be done about problems in the Church? For starters, parishes and dioceses must make reconciliation a priority, which means directing energy and resources toward it.

Here are a few things a parish might do to enhance its evangelization and reconciliation efforts:

- Establish an evangelization committee with reconciliation as a high priority.
- Develop an evangelization and reconciliation plan; communicate the plan and engage the entire parish in its implementation.

- Create detailed databases of target groups.
- Investigate existing effective reconciliation programs (ask your diocesan office of stewardship for help).
- Communicate regularly with *all* members, including those who are inactive.
- Identify parishioners who have special talents for and interest in reconciliation; train and support them in their work.
- Conduct a parish door-to-door census every five years.
- Periodically survey all members for feedback and input; publish the results and take appropriate action.

An excellent starting point is *A Time to Listen…A Time to Heal: A Resource Directory for Reaching Out to Inactive Catholics* published by the Committee on Evangelization of the National Conference of Catholic Bishops. Unfortunately, this booklet went out of print but still may be available through one of your diocesan offices. For information about the latest Catholic reconciliation materials, check the NCCB Web site at www.usccb.org.

The Christmas Machine

Each fall, U.S. retailers begin cranking up the infernal "Christmas Machine." Simultaneously, good Christians everywhere seek to drown out its noisy glitz with an ever-weakening protestation that "Jesus is the reason for the season." Sadly, Christians are not the only ones who are besieged by the annual Christmas merchandising juggernaut. Madison Avenue has ingeniously managed to drag the Jewish community into the Christmas morass by hyping a lesser Jewish feast, Hanukkah, as a Christmas surrogate.

There are certainly some benefits created in this country by the yearly Christmas marketing extravaganza: it provides jobs (someone must staff those annoying kiosks in the mall); it bolsters the economy (without Christmas retail sales, the U.S. economy would probably collapse!); people tend to be kinder (the idiocy of road rage decreases, although some people give guns as Christmas presents, perhaps in anticipation of the end of the holiday cease fire!); people are more generous (food pantries for the poor overflow at least until the new year begins); it lifts peoples' spirits (except those for whom Christmas is the saddest time of the year); it unleashes a flurry of overly sentimental TV "Christmas Specials" (a pleasant respite from gratuitous sex and violence, insipid sitcoms, and the scourge of whiny "reality TV" shows); and it reminds "C&E Catholics" that one of their two self-imposed holy days of obligation is approaching.

But the magnitude and pervasive impact of the Christmas machine—including the misinterpreted story of Saint Nicholas that begot the Santa Claus legend—is almost exclusively a North American phenomenon. Nowhere else in the world is one likely to find anything that resembles the manner in which the celebration of Christ's birth has been so grossly distorted. Perhaps we can put this into a stewardship perspective by quoting the following passage that recently made the rounds of parish bulletins and newsletters. Although it is not scientific, it is still an eye-opener to inequality in the world.

> If the earth's population were reduced to a village of only 100 people, with all human ratios remaining the same, there would be 57 Asians, 21 Europeans, 14 from North and South America, and 8 Africans. Seventy would be nonwhite and thirty white. Seventy would be non-Christian and thirty would be Christian.

> Fifty percent of the entire world's wealth would be in the hands of only six people, and all six would be in the United States. Seventy would be unable to read. Fifty would suffer from some degree of malnutrition. Eighty would be homeless or in substandard housing. Only one would have a college education.

In other words, 80 percent of the people in the world do not have a decent home; 70 percent cannot read; half of them do not get enough to eat; and, here in our country, we monopolize half the world's wealth.

As Christ's disciples, we're expected—required—to be grateful, responsible stewards of God's many blessings. One of God's most generous gifts is the decided privilege and, for most of us, the accidental circumstance of living in the United States. We can certainly try to avoid or ignore Christ's mandate to live as good stewards; but, as Christians, we can't deny it.

This year, as the flood of Christmas advertising is being released in all its fury, why not take time to review and evaluate your priorities and responsibilities as a U.S. citizen and Christian steward of God's gifts. It's conceivable that Jesus was anticipating a country like ours when, according to the writer of Luke's Gospel, he said: "From everyone to whom much has been given, much will be required; and from the one to whom much has been entrusted, even more will be demanded" (Luke 12:48).

The Parish Embrace

You may not remember the date—November 19, 1997—but many people can recall the event. Within a time span of just six minutes, Bobbi McCaughey, a resident of the village of Carlisle, Iowa, gave birth to the world's first known set of surviving septuplets. Not many days thereafter, another memorable event with more local significance took place in the suburbs of another Midwestern city. It didn't make international news headlines like the McCaughey septuplets, but it did stun the members of a particular rural Catholic parish. Three young people in their late teens and early twenties—two men and a woman—robbed a local convenience store. During the robbery, one member of the trio, whose family attended the rural Catholic parish, shot and killed the store's clerk.

In the wake of each of these unrelated incidences, something remarkably similar happened. The McCaughey family experienced an enormous outpouring of generosity from many quarters, including gifts of a new, bigger house and a lifetime supply of diapers. However, such acts of kindness are neither uncommon nor unexpected in the United States. What was truly astounding was the way the community of Carlisle, Iowa, particularly the congregation of the McCaugheys' church, quickly rallied around the young family. When Bobbi McCaughey finally brought her instant tribe home from the hospital, she found a small army of seventy volunteers waiting to help her and her husband care for the septuplets twenty-four hours a day, seven days a week.

Within minutes after the identity of the three people who had committed the convenience store robbery and murder was broadcast by the local news media, the distraught parents and grandparents of the shooter went to their parish church to seek God's comfort and guidance. To their astonishment, they found dozens of their fellow parishioners and their pastor waiting to pray with them and to console them.

On the flip side of these two inspirational occurrences is the sad story of a young woman who, like her two older siblings, was raised in a solid Catholic home and attended only Catholic schools. Shortly after beginning her career as a nurse, she met a young man with no religious background or church affiliation. They fell in love and were married. In her misguided attempt to accommodate her husband's indifference to religion, she stopped attending church and later made no effort to provide a religious upbringing for their two children.

While still in his early forties, the husband contracted an insidious form of leukemia. For two years, the family struggled with his illness, including a horrendous bone marrow transplant. Since she was a nurse, the wife served as the primary care giver throughout the ordeal. The couple's siblings and few friends, busy with their own families, provided what little assistance and comfort they could. However, because of the choices the couple had made, no parish family was available to come to their aid as happened in the first two instances above. When the husband eventually died, his wife became intensely embittered and soon severed all relationships with family and friends, including her own children, accusing them of not helping her cope with her husband's nightmarish illness.

What happened in the first two instances above, but not in the third, is a phenomenon this writer likes to call the "parish embrace." The parish embrace is common within church communities that have stepped onto a path leading to total stewardship. The members of total stewardship parishes recognize God as the source of all we have, and, in gratitude, commit themselves to furthering the word and work of Christ by caring for one another and all of God's creation. When parishioners become sensitized to God's great generosity, they look for opportunities to share their blessings with others. So it's not surprising that an entire stewardship-oriented community springs into action when one of its own is hurting or in need.

The quantity and quality of such a response is one measure of the progress of a community's stewardship conversion efforts. And it's a response that is not simply automatic or trivial. A grieving widow described her experience with the parish embrace like this: "When my husband suddenly died of a heart attack a few years ago, I was in complete shock. The hours I spent in the funeral home were like a blurry bad dream. All I remember is a stream of nondescript faces flowing past me saying how sorry they were. Weeks later, when I finally felt strong enough to look through the funeral home's guest book, I was flabbergasted by the names of the people who had signed it. I remembered almost none of them. What has deeply touched me since the funeral, however, are several of my fellow parishioners who, to this day, call regularly to see how I'm doing or invite me to spend time with them."

We live today in a highly mobile society that is no longer populated by multiple extended families who live, work, play, and pray together. In this disconnected cultural setting, church membership assumes even greater significance. Individuals and families who belong to stewardship-oriented parishes can take comfort in knowing that their parish family will wrap its collective arms around them if they ever need solace and support. There's no greater sign of God's presence than the loving embrace of a parish.

Stewardship's Tough Stuff

It was a cold, blustery Sunday morning in late winter in a big, northern city. An aged, weathered, bearded man was sitting on the ground, propped against the outside wall next to the main entrance of a large downtown church. He was leaning to one side, half reclining, appearing either drunk or asleep. His several layers of clothing were torn and tattered. His shoes were so worn that his bare toes were visible. He was surrounded by paper bags filled with his few earthly possessions.

As members of the congregation approached the church for Sunday services and caught sight of the wretched man, they visibly recoiled and gave him a wide berth as they entered the church. No one dared approach or speak to him. When the time came for the service to begin, the pastor, usually a very punctual person, was nowhere to be seen. The congregation buzzed and squirmed for about five minutes.

Suddenly the main door of the church opened and, to their surprise, the members of the congregation watched as the pitiable creature from the front of the church entered the building, slowly struggled down the center aisle and dragged himself into the sanctuary. He then turned around, faced the congregation, and slowly removed his old hat and beard. It was the pastor! He stood silent for a few seconds, which seemed like an eternity to the stunned congregation, then he moved to the podium, leaned into the microphone and said softly, "My dear fellow Christians, I believe we have something to talk about this morning. Perhaps it's time to review our discipleship."

Here are three citations, taken from documents recently promulgated by the Catholic bishops of the United States, which speak to the scene just described:

1. From their 1993 pastoral letter on evangelization, *Go and Make Disciples: A National Plan and Strategy for Catholic Evangelization in the United States:*

   Evangelization is the essential mission of the Church…evangelizing means bringing the Good News of Jesus into every human situation and seeking to convert individuals and society by the divine power of the Gospel (page 2)….The validity of our having accepted the Gospel does not only come from what we feel or…know; it comes also from the way we serve others, especially the poorest, the most marginal, the most hurting, the most defenseless, the least loved. An evangelization that stays inside ourselves is not an evangelization into the Good News of Jesus Christ (page 3).

2. From *A Shepherd's Care: Reflections on the Changing Role of Pastor* (USCCB Publishing 1987):

   While the "service model" of parish will remain the dominant one in growth areas, the need for an evangelizing or evangelical model will become even more intense in other parts of the country. In those areas where Catholic population is in decline, or where Catholic people are responding on a partial basis to the demands of the faith, pastors will inevitably be led to the development of more effective methods of outreach and evangelization. *Historically, Catholic pastors have not been strong evangelical ministers. In fact, many have shown a distinct distaste for this method of preaching and parish organization.* However, the fundamental changes in Catholic parish communities may well lead pastors to create distinctively Catholic forms of evangelization and outreach.

3. From the bishops' pastoral letter, *Stewardship: A Disciple's Response:*

    Every member of the Church is called to evangelize, and the practice of authentic Christian stewardship inevitably leads to evangelization (page 33).

    Evangelization and its "kissin' cousin" reconciliation are the "tough stuff" of stewardship conversion. What is your parish doing to attract new members, invite parishioners who have drifted away to return, and combat overt or subtle forms of bias, prejudice, and elitism? How successful are your parish's efforts to make welcome anyone who is different from the dominant social, ethnic, or economic group in your neighborhood?

STEP 4

Communication and Education

All the stewardship and development programs currently in use in dioceses and parishes throughout the United States require the use of one or more communications media. Printed material, audiovisuals, telemarketing programs, computerized tracking and record keeping, and other contemporary communications instruments now complement letters from the bishop or pastor, witness talks, bulletin announcements, posters, and other traditional means of communication.

Given the competition that exists today for people's time and attention, parishes and dioceses that wish to be successful in stewardship and development must pay careful attention to the effectiveness of their communications. Especially since most dioceses and parishes are working with very limited communications budgets, the choices that are made about how to "tell our story" or "make our case" can be crucial to success. With this in mind, parishes and dioceses are urged to seek the assistance of qualified communications professionals (staff and volunteers) to develop communications plans that will make the best possible use of available resources.

STEWARDSHIP: A DISCIPLE'S RESPONSE (PAGE 60)

Don't Confuse Me With the Facts

Most of us have had this experience: you're engaged in a dispute that revolves around a difference of recollection about specific facts or a particular event: a date, a place, certain people who were present, and so on. In an attempt to settle the dispute, someone determines the correct answer by researching an official source such as meeting minutes or newspaper articles. However, when the indisputable facts are presented to the parties involved, the person who held the contrary position refuses to accept them, thereby once again confirming the penetrating wisdom of the person who originally coined the phrase: "Don't confuse me with the facts!"

As mentioned earlier, for many decades, researchers have been intrigued by the fundamentally distinct operations of the human brain's two hemispheres. The left side of the brain handles analytical, data-processing functions—the "facts"—while the right side—the "global" side—is the domain of emotions and creative endeavors. Some scientists are convinced that people tend to be dominated by one side of their brain that, in the extreme, produces certain predictable behaviors and personality types. Ideally, human beings should strive to achieve an integrated balance between both brain hemispheres. Similarly, an ideal community is one that values and utilizes the gifts of both right- and left-brain-dominated members for the common good.

Parish stewardship conversion hinges on a collective change of heart, one that is more emotional and attitudinal (based on right-brain feelings) than logical and cognitive (based on left-brain facts). However, knowledge of concrete, reliable data can play a significant role in bringing parishioners to the brink of an emotion-driven decision to make a stewardship leap of faith. Therefore, parish leaders have a responsibility to systematically collect and communicate factual information to their fellow parishioners.

Communicating valid, reliable data on a regular basis provides a state-of-the-parish snapshot that parishioners can use to evaluate parish projects, programs, and services, gain insights into a parish's financial status, and measure the progress of stewardship conversion. In addition, keeping parishioners informed increases their sense of parish ownership, which is a vital component of the stewardship conversion process.

What kinds of statistics should be compiled and disseminated?

Some common data categories are financial (monthly or quarterly budget updates), demographic (number of parishioners, births, deaths, and new members), sociological (age groupings, educational backgrounds, income levels, and ethnic representations) and attitudinal (results of surveys about the parish and evaluations of parish programs and services). It's useful to track such data over time so that parish decision makers can use them for planning. It's also desirable to know where your parish fits into the big picture. Your diocesan stewardship and development office should be able to furnish diocesan totals against which to compare individual parish figures. Other excellent sources of comparative data are your friendly, local library and businesses in your area (banks, advertising agencies, news media, and so on), which have access to large national databases for marketing purposes.

Besides the items mentioned above, here are a few helpful facts to include in your data collecting activities:

- The number of collection envelopes distributed and used.
- Annual total offertory collections.
- Average annual collections per household.
- Average weekly mass attendance.
- Household giving as a percent of income.
- School expenses as a percent of total parish income (if a parish supports one or more schools).

When it comes to stewardship conversion, knowledge is indeed power. Parishioners who are being challenged to make stewardship a way of life need a comprehensive grasp of the condition of their parish. Hard numbers can help fill that need.

Please, Just Give Me a Sign!

Has this ever happened to you? You're scheduled to meet someone or attend a meeting at a place of business that is unfamiliar to you, and that consists of several buildings such as a school campus, a hospital complex, a Catholic parish, a factory, and so on. You approach the area and see several parking lots, none of which is marked for visitors. You park your car, get out, and see nothing that indicates where you should go. You enter the closest building and find several people engrossed in their work. You sheepishly approach the nearest person, excuse yourself, and ask for directions. The employee grunts something about a building at the other end of the property. You thank the employee for being so helpful, exit the building, and repeat the same process two or three times before you finally arrive at your meeting place. At this point you're probably harboring thoughts about this place of business that would make a sailor blush!

We can't stress often enough that a parish that is serious about its process of total stewardship conversion must be an hospitable place. Members and visitors alike should feel welcomed and accepted each time they encounter the parish, particularly through its staff members and volunteer leaders.

How welcoming is your parish or Catholic school?
It's not difficult to find out—just ask people who call or visit your facilities. Many first impressions of an organization are determined by how easily people can find their way from point A to point B.

One very common and easily corrected deficiency of hospitality involves something called "signage." Signage is the practice of displaying words and/or symbols in appropriate places to help people find what they are looking for. It's a combination of science and art focused on good communication. Attractive, effective signage is a major player in an organization's efforts to be welcoming and hospitable.

Hospitals are leading practitioners of top quality signage. The next time you visit a hospital, pay close attention to the manner in which you are directed by signs. The best signage systems will bring you to your destination without the inconvenience of asking for directions.

Many Catholic parishes and schools are woefully inadequate when it comes to signage. Parking areas, particularly those that double as school playgrounds, are unmarked. There are often no handicapped parking areas or spaces designated for staff members and visitors. In many instances, clearly visible signs for offices and directions to offices are non-existent, or they consist of tiny, weathered letters that were installed when buildings were constructed many years earlier. Meeting rooms and restrooms are frequently unmarked, particularly in buildings that have been converted from residences to activity centers. Visitors to many parishes and schools must wander around looking for someone to ask about the location of offices or meeting places. When people arrive for meetings, they often find no signs to direct them to meeting places, a situation aggravated when meetings are held in the evening and people must negotiate an unlit parking lot.

Testing the quality and adequacy of your signage is quite simple. Ask three or four people who are unfamiliar with your facilities to come to your location and try to find specific places: the pastor's residence, parish office, school principal's office, school library, a specific meeting room, and so on. You'll quickly learn how welcome people feel when they visit your parish or school. Be prepared for some unpleasant surprises.

"Did You Hear the One About...?"

A priest, a rabbi, and a minister walked into a bar. Upon noticing them, the bartender says: "Hey, is this some kinda joke?" At this point, dear reader, you are either laughing or you're at least beginning to realize *that* was a joke! In either case, God has blessed you with a most precious gift: a sense of humor.

We know from our own experiences that people can cheer us with humor when we're down in the dumps, or make us feel better with laughter when we're ill. Furthermore, the psychological and physiological benefits of humor are well documented. Norman Cousins, a former editor of *Saturday Review*, actually laughed himself to good health from an incurable disease, then wrote about his success in a milestone book, *Anatomy of an Illness as Perceived by the Patient* (1979).

So how does good humor relate to stewardship conversion?

After all, anything that has to do with our eternal salvation is serious business! However, we Christians sometimes tend to focus more on Calvary's suffering rather than on Easter's joy. Shouldn't our faith life be in sync with all of the elements and emotions of our humanity? Yes, there are no "outtakes" in the New Testament. But should we not believe that Jesus and his followers kidded one another, laughed, and shared funny stories whenever they were together?

We believe that we are sinners and, as such, we need occasional doses of guilt and remorse. But we also need heavy transfusions of optimism and inspiration to encourage and strengthen us on our journey as Christian disciples. Considering the amount of gloom and doom that assails us daily through the mass media, now, more than ever, we need our faith to help us "lighten up." Now, more than ever, we need to experience the Good News of Jesus Christ!

How about adding more inspiring stories, humorous anecdotes, and thrilling reports to parish bulletins, newsletters, and pulpit announcements? How about a renewed emphasis on liturgies that are intentionally planned to lift spirits? How about more homilies that touch hearts and make people smile or even laugh out loud? How about a serious review of the quality and effectiveness of parish hospitality and appreciation endeavors?

One of the last speeches of the late humorist Ogden Nash was a commencement address delivered at his granddaughter's 1970 high-school graduation (*The Atlantic Monthly*, June–July 2002). Regarding the role of humor within the human condition, Nash observed:

> Humor is not brash. It is not cheap. It is not heartless. Among other things, it is a shield, a weapon, a survival kit. So here we are, several million of us, crowded into our global concentration camp for the duration. How are we to survive? Solemnity is not the answer, any more than witless and irresponsible frivolousness. I think our best chance—a good chance—lies in humor, which, in this case, means a wry acceptance of our predicament.

The Mecca of Parish Stewardship

Perhaps you recall the visually stunning scene from the movie *Malcolm X*, or maybe you've seen one of the international news reports in March that show hundreds of thousands of white-robed followers of the Islamic faith slowly circling or kneeling to pray at the Ka'bah, the huge, cube-shaped structure in the center of Mecca's Grand Mosque. During a designated period each lunar year, more than two million Muslims perform their Haj—the pilgrimage to Mecca and neighboring Islamic holy places that Muslim men and women are required to make at least once during their lifetimes, if they are able. A visit to the Ka'bah is one of the Haj rituals.

When viewed from the air, the powerful image of thousands of circling, praying pilgrims clearly marks the Ka'bah as the epicenter of Islam's religious and spiritual universe. According to the Qur'an, the sacred scripture of Islam believed to have been revealed by God to the Prophet Muhammad in the Christian sixth century, the Ka'bah was built by Abraham and his son, Ishmael. Abraham instituted the Haj pilgrimage and established its rites that were later reestablished by Muhammad.

What do Catholics have that compares to the Ka'bah? Of course, there is a spiritual leader, the pope, whose physical presence in Rome creates a perception that Vatican City is the geographic hub of Catholicism. But Rome does not elicit the same intense emotional attraction among Catholics as does the Ka'bah in Mecca's Grand Mosque or the Dome of the Rock for Muslims or, for that matter, the Wailing Wall in Jerusalem for Jews.

In fact, Catholics don't need to journey to a distant land to find the ultimate place of worship and thanksgiving. A Catholic version of the Ka'bah can be found in every Catholic church. It's the altar upon which Christ's eucharistic sacrifice is recreated at each Mass. Furthermore, the success of parish stewardship conversion hinges on a parish's ability to make the Mass the axis on which the essence of the parish community revolves, analogous to the image of circling, praying Muslims at the Ka'bah. This can happen only if parish leaders truly want each Mass to replicate the life-altering moment the apostles experienced during the Last Supper. And this means spending more than a token amount of time and energy to prepare eucharistic celebrations. What parish leaders do not fantasize about a transcendent, Spirit-filled era in their parish's history, when all parishioners enthusiastically gather at Mass to worship and give thanks—not out of obligation but because of desire? Creating such a liturgical setting should be one of the principal goals of every parish engaged in stewardship conversion. A first step toward this goal would be an aggressive initiative involving more people more actively involved in parish liturgies, especially parishioners whose concept of "going to Mass" consists of passively watching a performance while executing perfunctory, low-impact aerobic sit-stand-kneel rituals.

Here's an example of an objective that could move a parish toward this goal: schedule every member—family or individual—to perform an active, public ministry during one of the weekend liturgies at least once a year. Adopting this objective will inspire liturgical planners to continually look for creative ways to engage all parishioners in the community's liturgies, and help motivate members to attend Mass because they feel connected to the celebration.

If we review the many different ministries that can be utilized at every Mass, it's easy to visualize a single annual role for every parishioner: choir members, cantors, lectors, servers, gift bearers, greeters, ushers, collection takers, decorators, parking lot attendants, transporters, musicians, and extraordinary communion ministers. (NOTE: Parish leaders must not overlook the importance of providing explicit job descriptions and sufficient training for *all* liturgical ministries.)

Here are few strategies that parishes have employed to achieve greater active liturgical participation:

1. Organize each ministry category (such as cantors or servers) into teams with a team leader. The leader is responsible for calling his/her team members a day or two before their scheduled tasks.
2. Schedule yearly appreciation dinners to honor and thank liturgical ministers for their faithful service.
3. Hold special annual or biannual commissioning ceremonies during Mass for all liturgical ministries.
4. Instead of, or in addition to, separate youth or childrens' liturgies, allow parish youngsters to perform suitable ministries during

weekend liturgies. For example, with training and direction, children can be excellent cantors and lectors and teens can assist with collection and serve as greeters.

5. Ask entire families to serve as gift bearers, compose offertory petitions, decorate the church, or serve at the altar.

6. Occasionally feature a different liturgical ministry in issues of the parish newsletter.

Increased participation in weekend liturgies will not happen simply because of goals and objectives. Parishioners must be regularly and personally invited to participate. To illustrate this point, here's what happened in one Midwestern parish. A talented and resourceful parishioner who, for many years, had served as the parish's unofficial "chief liturgical decorator" suddenly announced that she was retiring. For several months, the parish liturgy committee fretted about finding a suitable replacement. Finally, in frustration, the committee decided to issue a general call for help to the whole parish, even though the pastor repeatedly told the committee that "people in this parish just don't volunteer when you ask them to do something." At the close of every Mass on three successive weekends, one of the committee members made a public plea for volunteers to help with church decorations. By the end of the third weekend, twenty-seven people had volunteered! The clear message from this experience is: ask, and ask, and ask, and you will receive.

Another parish sought imaginative ways to engage parishioners in eucharistic celebrations. One of the women of the parish recommended an idea that eventually transformed her into a local celebrity known as the "flower lady." She identifies parishioners with flower gardens and asks them, from time to time, to donate some of their flowers to decorate the church. Each time the call for flowers is made, the response is overwhelming. The church is quickly filled with beautiful, fragrant blossoms and plants. The amateur florists are acknowledged during each Mass. Not only do they proudly attend Mass to see their green-thumb handiwork on display, they often bring friends and family members to celebrate with them.

What has your parish done lately that makes members look forward to the next time they celebrate the sacred mysteries?

Stewardship and Catholic Schools

From time to time, diocesan stewardship directors are questioned about the relationship between stewardship and Catholic schools. Many, but not all, of these inquiries are related to the stewardship of treasure. Here are a few FAQs (Frequently Asked Questions) about Catholic schools and stewardship:

Is Catholic school tuition part of my stewardship of treasure?
Christian stewardship of treasure refers to that portion of the financial blessings we have received from God that we return to God out of gratitude and that is used to continue Christ's work on earth. In most cases, tuition is simply payment for services rendered and, in fact, represents only a portion of the total cost of educating a student in a Catholic school.

Is Catholic school tuition tax deductible?
If payment to a Catholic school is indeed "tuition" as described above, the Internal Revenue Service does not consider it to be a charitable contribution and it is therefore not tax deductible.

I've heard that some parishes charge no tuition for their schools and in some cases even pay the high-school tuition for the children of their members. What's that all about?
Some parishes have chosen to operate as "total stewardship parishes." In these parishes, *all* parishioners are encouraged to tithe or give proportionately of their money to support *all* parish ministries, including Catholic schools. School families are not singled out from other parishioners for special treatment regarding their stewardship of treasure. Therefore, under certain conditions that are clearly spelled out by the Internal Revenue Service, contributions to a total stewardship parish are tax deductible. (NOTE: Your diocesan Office of Stewardship and Development or Treasurer's Office can provide the applicable IRS information.)

What is the actual annual cost of educating a child in a Catholic school?
Each Catholic school determines its own annual budget. There is no uniform budgetary standard. For example, the average annual cost per

student in the Catholic elementary schools in one Midwestern diocese for the 2003–2004 school year was about $3,500. These costs ranged from a high of $6,200 to a low of $2,600 per student.

Who pays the difference when tuition payments do not cover the actual cost?

In the case of parish elementary schools, the parish covers most of the difference from its ordinary operating income. Fundraising covers the rest. In the case of diocesan high schools, feeder parishes contribute a portion of the difference by means of what some call their "high school assessment." Again, fundraising activities and events cover the remainder.

What percentage of a parish's income is used to fund Catholic schools?

As mentioned above, each parish that supports a school is a unique case. On average, however, parishes in many dioceses with elementary schools spend about 75 percent of their total income on their own schools. In addition, some of these same parishes also contribute thousands of dollars to support neighboring Catholic high schools (see "high school assessment" above).

What are the responsibilities of parents who choose to send their children to Catholic schools?

Parents are the primary educators for their children. Without their active guidance and personal example, all efforts made by Catholic schools to form their children into responsible, faithful Catholic adults will often fail. Parents of Catholic school students must be prepared to support the efforts of their chosen school by living and practicing their own Catholic faith through such things as displaying solid Christian values in their personal and professional relationships, weekly Mass attendance, encouraging prayer in the home, involvement in parish activities, and being good stewards of their God-given gifts of time, talent, and treasure.

What about the quality of Catholic school education?

Catholic schools exist for two primary purposes: First, and foremost, to provide a Catholic spiritual and religious educational environment that produces young men and women who are well grounded in the Catholic faith, who choose to practice their faith throughout their lifetimes, and who are ready and willing to actively participate in their parishes and dioceses as adults.

Second, to provide exemplary academic and social development programs that prepare students to become responsible, productive members of society in their homes, in their workplaces, and in their communities.

The justification for continuing to expend the lion's share of a parish's resources for its Catholic school hinges on a realistic, positive evaluation of these two purposes. One critical question that proponents and supporters of Catholic schools must constantly ask is: Is the Catholic Church getting its money's worth? Are Catholic schools producing young Catholic men and women who will be faithful practicing Catholics and eventually become leaders, or at least strongly supportive members, of their parishes wherever their parishes may be located when they become independent adults?

Successories

If you're engaged in any aspect of leadership, either a professional or a volunteer, you may have received one of the mail-order catalogs that feature motivational items such as pictures, plaques, and other novelties. Or you may have wandered through one of those little franchise shops named "Successories" that are found in many malls. In any case, you've been exposed to an array of sage quotations that some people believe will make them and their organizations successful if they hang them on their walls. To be sure, many of these sayings are quite insightful and can indeed make a difference if taken to heart: "Your attitude determines your altitude," "Working together means winning together," "The person on the top of the mountain didn't fall there," and so on.

We can't emphasize enough that a stewardship parish is a community that values outstanding service and promotes extraordinary hospitality. Some of the successories-type slogans, particularly those that refer to customer service, speak volumes to any parish involved in stewardship conversion. Consider, if you will, these examples in relationship to your own parish (we've altered them slightly by substituting "parishioner" and "parish" for "customer" and "company"):

- *"It takes months to find a parishioner…seconds to lose one."* No matter how faithful and devoted parishioners may be, one cruel remark or unkind act by the pastor or staff member is sometimes enough to drive them away.
- *"Parishioner complaints are the schoolbooks from which we learn."* Yes, parishioners can also at times be unkind and insensitive. But many of their critical observations may be accurate and call for changes or improvements.
- *"The golden rule for every parish is this: Put yourself in the parishioner's place."* What does the parish truly look like through the eyes of an average member? Do parish leaders regularly solicit input about parish life from parishioners?
- *"The parishioner is our final inspector."* In the last analysis, the parish belongs to the parishioners. The Church's own book of laws defines a parish as "a definite community of the Christian faithful established on a stable basis within a particular church…" (Canon 515). The main responsibility of pastors and staff members is to serve and provide pastoral care for parishioners.
- *"Rule #1: If we don't take care of our parishioners, somebody else will."* The implications of this motto are painfully obvious. How many names appear on your parish membership list? How many of the people on that list do you see at Mass each weekend? Over the years, how many members of your parish or neighboring parishes have shifted their membership to other denominations, or to no church at all?

If your parish is truly serious about stewardship conversion, here are two additional successories quotes you might tack on parish walls:

- *"Perfection is our goal. Excellence will be tolerated."*
- *"Even if you're on the right track, you'll get run over if you just sit there."*

STEP 5

Affirming Gifts
of Time and Talent

The demands made on people's time and energy make it more important than ever to recruit, train, and recognize gifts of time and talent for the parish or diocese. Active recruitment of volunteers is essential to the parish's and diocese's stewardship of its own human and financial resources because the active involvement of individuals, families, and communities in the mission and ministries of the Church is one of the surest signs of the vitality of any faith community.

To make sure that the time and talent of volunteers are respected and used wisely, dioceses and parishes should invest staff time and budget resources in the training and continuing education of volunteers. They should also find appropriate ways to recognize and celebrate the precious gifts of time and talent that people contribute to the Church on behalf of the mission of the Church.

New educational resources and training materials are needed to help parishes and dioceses improve their efforts to recruit, train, and recognize volunteers. To ensure that gifts of time and talent receive their proper emphasis and are not overshadowed by efforts to secure gifts of treasure, careful attention should be paid to this important aspect of a total stewardship education program.

STEWARDSHIP: A DISCIPLE'S RESPONSE (PAGES 60–61)

Stewardship's Three Little Words

Reform movements have a way of producing unique jargon and buzzwords. The current stewardship conversion movement within the North American Catholic Church is no exception. Time, talent, and treasure are three words that, when used in tandem, immediately evoke the concept of Christian stewardship. Time, talent, and treasure encompass all of God's gifts to us, a portion of which good stewards are expected to return to God in gratitude. Let's take a closer look at what it means to be good stewards of time and talent.

Stewardship of Time

What is more precious to us than our time? Certainly not money, which we never seem to have enough of anyway! Not even family or friends are more important because, without time, we would not be able to love and enjoy them. After all, don't people sometimes say: "I cherish nothing more than the time I spend with those I love!" As we grow older, we tend to become more protective of our time, perhaps because we're increasingly aware of the limited amount we have.

For Christians, time is simply a way to measure God's great gift of life. As disciples of Jesus Christ, we're aware of our obligation to be good stewards of our time and, indeed, of all the blessings God has bestowed on us. Among other things, this includes giving back to God a portion of our time to help build God's kingdom on earth.

How much time do we have to return to God? Let's review the numbers. There are 8,760 hours in a 365-day year. Sleeping eight hours a day reduces our conscious hours by 2,920 annually, leaving 5,840. Working 40 hours per week outside the home (less two vacation weeks) reduces the time over which we have more or less control by another 2,000 hours, leaving 3,840. We won't even attempt to calculate the countless hours stay-at-home parents spend on chores and child care! Factor in a 1-hour commute, throw in 3 hours a day for meals and personal grooming, and we wind up with 2,495 hours we might call our "discretionary time."

Watching two hours of television each day (only the most sophisticated, cultural channels of course!) reduces our annual discretionary time to 1,765, leaving about 4 to 5 hours a day to do things like shopping, hobbies, shuttling kids, visiting relatives and friends, deleting e-mail "spam," napping, doing laundry, paying bills, answering telemarketing phone calls, opening junk mail, fixing a leaky toilet, surfing the Internet, going to church—and practicing good stewardship!

How we choose to share our discretionary time is a personal exercise in setting priorities, and is generally our response to such questions as: What do I feel **obligated** to do? What do I **want** to do? What do I **like** to do? What gives me some return on my time investment? Does anyone recognize and appreciate my efforts?

The premier stewardship of time challenge for a parish engaged in stewardship conversion is determining ways to "bump" parish needs and activities to the top of parishioners' priority lists. In an increasingly hectic world, parishes compete with the "business of busyness," that is, the perception that people have precious little time to spare, even with all of the time-saving devices now available to us. The real task for parish leaders is to help members understand the difference between "doing the job right" and "doing the right job" in their lives, and connecting with them in a way that motivates them to want to return some of God's time for God's work.

Stewardship of Talent

We see it with increasing regularity: a runner carries a football into the end zone for a touchdown and, in the midst of cheering and celebration, drops to one knee for a silent prayer. A movie star or popular musician is called to the stage to receive a prestigious award and begins the obligatory litany of "thank yous" by saying: "First of all I want to thank God for having blessed my life."

It's certainly refreshing when talented celebrities publicly recognize their dependence on God's generosity. Yet many famous people behave as though their superior physical prowess or exceptional artistic talents somehow originate from their own efforts. Through a unique and mysterious confluence of genetics and environment, one person paints masterpieces, another writes epics, another composes symphonies, while still others run faster, jump higher, or grow stronger than ordinary humans.

To be sure, hard work, dedication, and personal effort are often required to develop native talent. Disciples of Jesus Christ know that the basic human traits from which all these extraordinary accomplishments flow are unearned gifts from God, the source of all. We are simply caretakers of God's gifts.

When we lend someone a prized possession, we assume it will be returned in at least the same condition as it was when we lent it. We would normally expect some expression of appreciation for our generosity. And it would be reasonable to think that the person to whom we lent our property might offer some sort of favor in return. God is the divine lender. During our earthly sojourn, we're allowed temporary use of God's belongings. Christ's good and bad steward parables remind us of our obligation to be responsible and accountable recipients of God's gifts and that the "Master" expects some reasonable return on his investment as an expression of our gratitude.

Before we can gratefully return a portion of our talents to God, we must first identify and own them. So often we hear people say: "Oh, I have no particular talents" or "I'm just an average person; there's nothing I do all that well." When people accomplish something extraordinary, they frequently deflect praise by saying: "Oh, it's not that good"; "I guess I was just lucky," and so on.

In a world frequently subjected to braggarts and blowhards, self-effacing humility can be a welcome relief. But God does not breathe a life into us that is totally devoid of abilities, skills, talents, and interests. Saint Paul was absolutely correct. "For as in one body we have many members, and not all the members have the same function, so we, who are many, are one body in Christ, and individually we are members one of another. We have gifts that differ according to the grace given to us: prophecy, in proportion to faith" (Romans 12:4–6). Everyone receives a unique array of God's gifts. The challenge for disciples of Jesus Christ is to discover those gifts, develop them, and return a portion to God in gratitude.

Here are some questions we can ask ourselves to help identify our talents, interests, and abilities:

1. What is my occupation, vocation, or profession?
2. What additional skills, talents, or interests do I have?
3. What are my spare time hobbies?
4. What kinds of skills, talents, or abilities do my friends and family members tell me I have?
5. What are some specific needs in my community that I know I could help meet?

Some people may have difficulty acknowledging their talents. Many Catholics were taught that disclosing their exceptional abilities constitutes a sin of pride. Yet we have repeatedly heard Christ's admonition to let our lights "shine before others, so that they may see your good works and give glory to your Father in heaven" (Matthew 5:16). Parish leaders may have to help some parishioners understand that it's OK to be justifiably proud of the special gifts God has entrusted to their care.

How we return talents to God can be somewhat perplexing. Unlike time and money, talents are difficult to quantify and therefore do not easily lend themselves to a strict application of a concept like tithing. Perhaps it has to do with the amount of risk, the level of intensity, the degree of difficulty, or the magnitude of sacrifice, none of which can be measured in dollars and cents or by a clock. The person who struggles to give three hours a week to clean the church may be returning the same amount of talent and quality time to God as the person who meets three hours a month as a member of the parish council. However, as we become increasingly aware of our abilities, Christ's words make even more sense: "From the one to whom much has been entrusted, even more will be demanded" (Luke 12:48).

Returning time, talent, and treasure to God has been described as "taking our hands off of some of God's possessions." God has assured us that, in every case, the results will be spiritually enriching and emotionally satisfying.

Energizing Events or Wasted Opportunities?

When was the last time you made or heard one of these remarks about the eucharistic celebrations in your parish?

"Gee, Father, I love your sermons, but they're way too short." "Hurry up, Mom and Dad, we (kids) can't wait to get to church!" "What a shame that Mass lasted only an hour and a half this morning." "I so look forward to going to church every weekend, and when I'm there, I just hate to leave." "I know there's a big game on television this afternoon, but I'd much rather go to Mass."

Or does this sound more familiar? "I had my stopwatch on Father's homily this morning. It lasted almost fifteen minutes!" "Aw, Mom, do we *have* to go to church today?" "Come on, Martha, let's get out of here now so we can beat the crowd out of the parking lot." "I really don't feel like going to church today; let's just skip it this week."

There are probably some Catholic parishes where the first group of comments above can be overheard. There are undoubtedly many parishes where the second group is more common.

Catholics are taught to believe that each celebration of the holy Eucharist is a reenactment of the Last Supper. Do you suppose any of the apostles—other than Judas—really didn't want to be in that upper room with Jesus? When early Christians gathered secretly in the catacombs to celebrate the Eucharist and strengthen their resolve against their Roman persecutors, do you think they were the least bit concerned about how long the services lasted? When the first Catholic immigrants came to the United States in search of religious freedom and a better life, could anyone doubt that their liturgical gatherings were the focal points of the life of their parish communities?

What has happened to the excitement and spirit that characterized these and other early Catholic groups? Why do so many Catholics approach weekend liturgies with negative attitudes, if they attend at all? The answer is as complex as each person's own experiences with "church." For some, it's boring liturgies and homilies; for others, it's celebrants who seem to go through the motions quickly just to "get it over with." For some, its lethargic music and embarrassingly inept singing; for still others, it's years of parents and teachers enforcing an oppressive obligation rather than emphasizing a joyful opportunity. For many young people today, it's the influence of the entertainment media. All of these elements—and many more—potentially converge to drive a wedge between the blessed celebration of Christ's redemptive act and the manner in which it actually transpires each week in our churches.

How should parish leaders respond when they find indifference and even hostility toward the premier sacred action that should be the spiritual and inspirational centerpiece of parish life? We suggest three words: assessment, planning, and feedback.

> *Assessment:* ask members what they think contributes to any negative feelings toward the eucharistic liturgies in the parish.
>
> *Planning:* use the data from the assessment to make appropriate and necessary changes or improvements.
>
> *Feedback:* institute a regular, systematic means of soliciting input from parishioners about how things are going.

Here's a helpful tip for all Catholics who long for better parish liturgies: when you attend Mass in other locales, note the customs and practices that impress you. Share your discoveries with your parish leaders. If they're effective and capable leaders, they'll be open to ways to improve liturgical celebrations.

The celebration of the Eucharist is the pivotal weekly event for parishes committed to the process of stewardship conversion. Each uninspired and uninspiring parish liturgy is a wasted opportunity to energize parishioners on their stewardship journeys.

Do You Love Me? The Tevye Quandary

If you've seen the movie or stage production of *Fiddler on the Roof*, you may recall the scene when the lead character, Tevye, musically asks his wife, Golde, the ultimate spousal question: "Do you love me?" (their marriage, twenty-five years earlier, had been arranged; they met each other for the first time on their wedding day).

Golde is obviously caught off-guard by the question, so her initial reaction is more of an attempt to cope with her surprise than it is a reply to Tevye. As she tries to compose herself, she simply reflects his question by saying: "Do I love you?" Tevye presses her for a yes-or-no response, but Golde, still unnerved, proceeds to enumerate everything she has done for him during their marriage: wash his clothes, cook his food, give him children, and so on. But this is not enough for Tevye; he continues to prod for a definite answer. Finally, after considering all they have endured during their years together, Golde and Tevye tenderly conclude that they must, indeed, love each other.

Parishioners and parish staff members often experience a version of the Tevye Quandary when dealing with parish leadership. Some pastors, parish life coordinators, pastoral associates, deacons, school principals, parish directors of religious education, and other assorted parish leaders often fall short when it comes to telling volunteers and staff members how important they are for the life of the parish, and that their good works and support are appreciated. Someone once observed that leaders who neglect to express praise and gratitude might be subconsciously saying: "No one ever thanks me or tells me how much my work is needed, so why should I tell others?"

Let's consider the Tevye Quandary from the viewpoints of both leaders and their constituents. A confident, competent leader is self-affirming; he or she does not require the adulation of others in order to be motivated. Yes, it's certainly pleasant to be praised and thanked, but proficient leaders don't need the acclaim of others, nor do they expect it or seek it. (When was the last time you heard highly respected leaders attempt to elicit sympathy by complaining about how "busy" they are? Great leaders don't have to tell others how hard they work. They simply do what must be done!)

Subordinates, on the other hand, desperately need to hear from their superiors how well they're doing, and that what they do is important and appreciated. A steady diet of positive, helpful feedback from those in authority is a required ingredient for successful and productive leader/follower relationships.

Unfortunately, we often hear reports of statements like these made by authority figures, including parish and other Church leaders:

"My people are paid well to do their jobs. What more do they expect of me?"

"I'm just not the kind of person who goes around telling people how much I appreciate them. They should know how I feel."

"I'm not good at praising people for their work. It's just not my style."

We also hear frequent comments about "Yes, but" managers. This group may occasionally express praise and/or appreciation—albeit faint—but it must always be conditioned with a criticism: "You did a fairly good job with that project, but I didn't like…" Finally, there are those completely miscast bosses whose only feedback consists of finding fault and criticizing. Their insecurity causes them to believe they will somehow diminish themselves by praising others, a syndrome rendering them incapable of truly effective leadership.

The fact remains that most of us who are striving to live as good Christian stewards need to hear occasional positive, uplifting, motivating, appreciative comments from our Church leaders. Students of human nature generally agree that when desirable behavior is not reinforced, it will deteriorate. In the best stewardship parishes and dioceses, there is a climate of cooperation, trust, celebration, and appreciation. Ideas and talents are valued. Leaders are committed to strategies that identify and use the skills and abilities of the members of their communities, even as they search for ways to manage or strengthen community weaknesses.

What's the current status of gratitude and encouragement in your parish? Does your parish have a systematic means of discovering and celebrating the charisms of each parishioner? How, and how often, are people recognized for their generous gifts of time, talent, and treasure? When gratitude is expressed, is it sincere?

Beginning with its leaders, every parish should, from time to time, evaluate its systems and structures regarding the ways it reinforces and encourages the good works of its parishioners. If you're not sure how to do this, find a couple of business marketing specialists in your area. They'll show you how to use some of their clever tools. Remember always that what we do is for God's greater honor and glory as we search for more and better ways to spread Christ's Good News.

Parish Ministry Fair:
A Party With a Purpose

If you're looking for a marvelous way to inject some life into your parish's volunteer activities, try a Parish Ministry Fair. A Ministry Fair is an annual celebration of Time and Talent Stewardship—a major parish party with a multitude of benefits.

A Parish Ministry Fair is an opportunity for every parish club, group, or organization to showcase its work to the entire parish. It usually takes place after all Masses on a selected weekend. The event should be held in a space large enough for each volunteer group to have its own display area, such as a gymnasium or large cafeteria, plus room for parishioners to roam easily among the exhibits.

Here are just a few of the benefits of a well-organized Parish Ministry Fair:

- It gives volunteers a chance to show off the good works they perform for the parish (a little well-placed pride is a great motivator).
- It highlights the stewardship message that we express our gratitude to God for the blessings we have received by giving some of our time and talent back to God.
- It provides valuable education and information about what's happening in the parish, and what's available for parishioners who want to get involved.
- It creates another occasion for parishioners to come together to celebrate, and to get to know one another.
- It allows the parish community to recognize and thank people for their many hours of selfless volunteer work within the parish.
- It provides an excellent opportunity for parish clubs and organizations to recruit new volunteers for their endeavors.

The success of a Ministry Fair hinges on these factors:

- The enthusiasm of the pastor and parish leaders. The pastor, staff and key parishioners must be excited about this, or any other parish activity, to ensure its success.

- Adequate planning and careful timing. Every parish group needs to "own" the event and participate in its planning. Careful thought should be given to selecting the best time of year for the fair aimed at getting the highest attendance of possible volunteers.
- Abundant promotion. There's no good substitute for aggressively advertising the event through every conceivable medium of communication available to the parish: newsletters, bulletins, posters, pulpit announcements, or direct-mail invitations. If you sell it well, they will come!
- Stress the FUN! When you attend a fair, you expect to have a good time. True to its name, a Ministry Fair should be a parish party with plenty of hospitality in a fun atmosphere. Among other things, this means light refreshments, colorful decorations, and unobtrusive music (not too loud, so visitors and volunteers at each exhibit can converse without shouting).
- Follow-up. Be sure that anyone who "signs-up" for one or more of the featured organizations or activities is contacted within a week.

If any parishes in your area already have ministry fairs, check them out, and invite their fair planners to attend yours.

Contact your local diocesan stewardship office for more information about how to conduct a successful ministry fair.

The Switched-On Parish

We can't say it often enough: Christian stewards profess to believe that God is the source of all gifts and talents. It follows, then, that human inventions are simply manifestations of God at work through man's creative giftedness. So why not employ some of today's man-made technologies when they can promote personal stewardship, reinforce a parish's spirit of hospitality and welcoming, or anything else that would improve the spiritual life of a parish community?

One example of new technologies that is finding a valuable place in church settings is video equipment. Some parishes have installed video projection and taping equipment in their churches as both a tool for enhancing liturgical celebrations and in reaction to aggressive professional and amateur photographers and videographers who tend to swarm over and disrupt sacred events. The final straw for one pastor was the "wedding planner" whose videographer planted numerous portable floodlight stands throughout the sanctuary and also ruined the church's carefully calibrated audio system.

On the other hand, savvy parish leaders see several beneficial uses of videotaping capabilities. A well-designed and properly operated videotaping system can produce a professional-quality, immediately-available keepsake record of any event that takes place in church, such as weddings, funerals, first communions, confirmations, graduations, and other special parish and family celebrations. It's also an excellent tool for evaluating liturgies. Some parish leaders may find this latter use a bit threatening, but it can have a dramatic positive effect on the way parishes celebrate the sacred mysteries and conduct other events in church. And what stewardship-based parish doesn't want to continually improve its liturgies?

Here are several issues to consider before installing a videotape system in your church:

1. Take the time and make the effort to educate the parish community about the value and benefits of a videotaping/video projection system before it's installed; demonstrate its capabilities when it becomes fully operational.
2. Don't skimp on equipment. Invest in good quality color digital surveillance cameras ("broadcast quality" cameras are an unnecessary extravagance). Complete the setup with peripheral mechanical and electronic components that include a professional-style control board capable of being operated by one person.
3. A good video system should be linked to a top notch sound system that includes adequate "miking" of all sound-producing areas and individuals.
4. Two principles should govern the placement of cameras:

† They should be permanently mounted in areas where they are unobtrusive. In many churches this will call for some creative positioning. However, good video cameras are now quite small and lightweight, which makes concealling them much easier.

† They should have pan-tilt-zoom capabilities to produce full coverage of the church for any event. In most churches, four cameras would provide maximum coverage: one in the back of the sanctuary facing the congregation, one on either side at the entrance of the sanctuary or apse, and one in the back of the church which can capture the nave, main aisle, and sanctuary and swivel 180 degrees to see the gathering area and main entrance. In smaller churches, one of the two side cameras could be eliminated without seriously effecting the coverage of most events.

6. Several parishioners should be trained to competently operate the system.

The cost of a good quality videotaping system depends on several factors, some of which are dictated by the local economy. However, you should expect to spend somewhere between $12,000 and $15,000 range for hardware and an additional $10,000 to $15,000 for professional installation. This is indeed a hefty investment, but one which will more than pay for itself in good will and beneficial uses.

Myths and Stewardship

Not long ago, John Stossel, a reporter best known for his "Give Me a Break" segments on the ABC news magazine *20/20*, presented a one-hour primetime special entitled "Lies, Myths, and Downright Stupidity." His premise was that many Americans harbor certain stereotypical beliefs and opinions that are completely unsupported by empirical data. At least two of the items on Stossel's list have a direct bearing on parish efforts to promote stewardship as a way of life. They are: "We have less free time than we used to" and "American families need two in-comes."

Regarding "less free time," many Americans incessantly express the feeling that they are overwhelmed by their "busy" schedules and are con-stantly pressed for time. Yet when researchers asked people to keep time diaries in order to calculate how much free time they really have, they discovered "a discrepancy between what people say and what they re-port." In fact, researchers found that people actually have almost twice as much free time as they estimate—and certainly much more free time than people had twenty or thirty years ago.

Steve Moore, coauthor of *Things Are Getting Better All the Time,* says, "One of the reasons that Americans feel so pressed for time is there's so much more to do in life today." For example, one of the most popular pastimes is watching television. If a person watches an average of two hours a day—one half hour of local news, one half hour of national news, and either two half-hour sitcoms or one hour-long drama—that amounts to thirty 24-hour days of television viewing per year. In other words, you are watching television nonstop for one entire month!

Regarding the "need for two incomes," Stossel found that this per-ception was driven by the desire for "more and better stuff." The U.S. Department of Commerce reports that, even after accounting for infla-tion, personal disposable income has tripled over the past fifty years. For example, fifty years ago, the average family in the U.S. had one car. To-day the norm is two or three. Houses have more than doubled in square footage, and shoppers "just seem to spend as much as they want." As author Moore points out: "Most families don't have to have both par-ents working. They do this by choice. People have decided they want to maintain a very high income lifestyle on two incomes to have all the things to keep up with the Joneses."

People always seem to find the time and the money to spend on those things that they consider to be life's "priorities." The challenge for a parish engaged in a process of stewardship conversion is finding ways to motivate people to joyfully and gratefully embrace their responsibili-ties as disciples of Jesus Christ that will, in turn, stimulate them to assess and reorder their time, talent, and treasure priorities.

STEP 6

Stewardship
of Treasure

Parishes and dioceses that wish to encourage financial gifts for on-going programs, capital needs, and endowment should look first to the previous five steps.

- *Has the parish or diocese effectively witnessed to the value of stewardship as a way of life?*
- *Is the leadership fully committed to stewardship and development?*
- *Are individuals and families in this diocese or parish actively involved in ministries of hospitality, evangelization, and service?*
- *How effective are parish or diocesan communications?*
- *And, finally, are gifts of time and talent really welcome, or does the parish or diocese unwittingly send a message that it only cares about money?*

The parish or diocese that can honestly evaluate itself on these questions with a positive result will be in an excellent position to encourage gifts of treasure to support the mission and ministries of the Church. Building on this kind of solid foundation, the diocese or parish should employ fundraising methods that respect and reinforce stewardship themes of gratitude, accountability, generosity, and returning to the Lord with increase.

Within a total stewardship context, parishes and dioceses should not hesitate to use the best available ethically sound fundraising practices to ask the Catholic people to make financial contributions that are planned, proportionate, and sacrificial. Provided that the basic approach is consistent with the theology and practice of stewardship, the principles and techniques of professional fund raising can be extremely helpful to the overall stewardship and development efforts of the parish or diocese.

STEWARDSHIP: A DISCIPLE'S RESPONSE (PAGE 61)

Stewardship of Treasure

We've said it before, but it merits repetition: living a stewardship way of life is unfamiliar territory for most of today's cradle Catholics. Recent generations of Catholics have drifted away from the commitment to total stewardship that characterized our ancestors—a phenomenon that is most apparent when we assess the current status of stewardship of treasure in the United States. Charitable financial gifts to mainline Christian churches are steadily declining and, particularly among Catholics, the practice of tithing is a novelty, something Catholics are not accustomed to, not a standard.

There's an eternal truth associated with the stewardship of treasure: it can be a swift and brutal measure of the quality of parish life. Stewardship of treasure, as reflected in weekend collections and other monetary contributions, is an extraordinarily sensitive bellwether of the disposition of a parish family. **Parishioners cast their votes with their checkbooks.** We know the usual things that can positively or negatively impact parish income: poor homilies, uninspired and uninspiring liturgies, substandard service, disagreements with Church teachings, ineffective pastoral leadership, incompetent parish or school staff members, and any local decision that requires spending money, making a change, or taking action! But there are also trivial, "you've-got-to-be-kidding!" circumstances that cause people to leave the parish or at least stop contributing. This, of course, includes any decision that requires spending money, making a change, or taking action!

Stewardship of treasure is also an excellent indicator of the progress of a parish's stewardship conversion efforts. People who truly own their parish, and whose parish serves their spiritual and temporal needs well, are more open to the practice of tithing or proportional giving (see below). They are also much more willing to share their time and talent than are alienated or marginalized parishioners.

True believers, agnostics, and atheists all agree: we'll never escape this life alive. Furthermore, we enter the world with nothing and, with the rare exception of a few emotionally skewed individuals who are buried in their favorite automobiles or surrounded by their jewelry collections, we exit with nothing. Whatever we accumulate during our passage through time is temporarily on-loan, notwithstanding this message seen on the marquee of a California bank located across from a cemetery: "Deposit your money with us; you can't take it with you, but you can keep it close!"

Christians profess to believe that God is the master who owns everything and generously allows us, the stewards, to use certain things during our mortal journey. In practice, however, many Christians seem to stumble over the phrase: "God is the source of everything." Some might respond to that with: "After all, don't we work hard to provide for ourselves and our families?" But even the very talents and abilities we use to make a living—beginning with life itself—are also God's gifts! We are the caretakers of God's property. Our salvation depends on the quality of our stewardship.

Tithing is the traditional cornerstone of stewardship of treasure. It's relatively easy to understand, but not so easy to promote and practice. The mandate for God's people to tithe is rooted in the Old Testament: "Set apart a tithe of all the yield of your seed that is brought in yearly from the field" (Deuteronomy 14:22); "the choicest of the first fruits of your ground you shall bring into the house of the LORD your God. You shall not boil a kid in its mother's milk" (Exodus 23:19); " of all that you give me I will surely give one tenth to you" (Genesis 28:22). "First fruits" in today's vernacular is 10 percent of gross earnings or, in IRS terminology, adjusted gross income (AGI).

We noted elsewhere that, on average, American Catholics contribute less than 2 percent of their annual incomes to the Church. The nature of today's economy, coupled with societal pressures and lifestyle choices, makes the decision to tithe a heroic one for many Christians, particularly young families struggling with mortgages, car payments, insurance premiums, student loans, taxes, raising children, and so on. Yet, in spite of the great sacrifice required, a growing number of Catholics are embracing the tithe, and are experiencing many blessings and much peace as a result.

Furthermore, many parish priests are overcoming their reluctance to "talk tithing." They are also choosing to tithe as a model for their parishioners. We should mention, however, that priests who claim to tithe often do so based on their salaries. Salaries for diocesan priests are determined by each diocese, but are not ordinarily accurate reflections of the total cost of a priest's lifestyle. Many expenses that laypeople must pay from their own incomes (housing, furnishings, utilities, social security payments, health insurance, disability insurance, and retirement plans) are provided for priests. A priest who tithes on his take-home paycheck is not tithing on the same gross income as a salaried or wage-earning layperson–a point he should consider before asking his parishioners to join him in tithing.

"Proportional giving" is tithing's stewardship of treasure economically friendlier cousin. Proportional giving, like tithing, is an intentional decision to return to God a fixed percentage of annual gross income. The actual amount—typically less than 10 percent—is an annual "floating percentage" based on personal circumstances. Many Catholics employ proportional giving as a strategy for moving toward a full tithe. They first calculate their current percent-of-income giving, then increase their giving by one or two percentage points each year until they have reached the full tithe.

What's the Payoff?

Good stewards don't "give to get." The fundamental stewardship of treasure motivation for Christians should be gratitude for the many gifts God has given us. We are, after all, simply returning a portion of God's own possessions! For most Christians, the decision to tithe or give proportionately is simply a matter of rearranging financial and lifestyle priorities, and learning how to separate "needs" from "wants."

There is, however, a marvelous payoff for good stewardship. One veteran Christian steward described it like this: "Ever since I accepted Christ's stewardship mandate, I've become highly sensitized to the many blessings God pours over me and my family every day, so many things I used to take for granted. It's overwhelming! I can't begin to thank God enough. Even giving back 10 percent seems puny compared to what God has given me!"

Fundraising 101

It can't be stated too forcefully or too often: stewardship is not a synonym for fundraising, nor are parish stewardship conversion efforts simply a devious way to extract more money from Catholic parishioners by sugarcoating fundraising with theology and sacred Scripture. The practical rewards and spiritual value of the stewardships of time and talent are as great as, if not greater than, those of the stewardship of treasure.

But we must also be honest and realistic. Living a stewardship way of life does, indeed, require grateful generosity with our money as well as with our time and talent. Returning a sacrificial portion of my income to God, in gratitude for the many gifts and blessings I have received, is certainly one tangible measure of my desire to be a good steward.

There is, in fact, a hand-in-glove relationship between the stewardship of treasure and the successful strategies and productive techniques of the professional enterprise known as fundraising. Fundraising is not unique to the United States. However, no other country can match the exceptional sophistication of U.S. fundraisers' tactics to cultivate charitable giving and promote philanthropy. And no other country can match the extraordinary generosity of the American people when called upon to help others in need.

What, exactly, is fundraising? An experienced fundraiser once described his occupation like this: "No matter how impressive my organizational title as a fundraiser may sound, I'm basically a salesman." He came to this insight after reading an article listing the ten cardinal rules for a successful salesperson. He noticed that his professional activities were based on the same rules. Because leaders of parishes engaged in a process of stewardship conversion should have more than just a superficial understanding of the fundamentals of successful fundraising, let's review those ten rules—substituting the words *donor* or *parishioner* for *buyer*, and *fundraiser* for *salesperson*—and see how they can be used to maximize parish efforts to foster good stewardship of treasure:

1. *Think Like a Donor:* Parishioners support their parishes with time, talent, and treasure because they are convinced they are making an investment in a worthy organization. In return, they want respect, honesty, and a feeling of confidence that the parish is fulfilling its mission and serving their needs.

2. *Be Considerate:* Parishioners will give generously if they experience parish leaders as competent, caring people (most donors give to people, not causes). Parish leaders and staff members demonstrate competence and caring through their communication and interaction with parishioners. Simple things like a smile, eye contact, a firm handshake, appropriate hugs, and straight talk tell parishioners that they are cherished members of their parish.

3. *Offer Service:* One of the hallmarks of a stewardship parish is value-added service, that is, service that goes beyond simply what is required. This demands extra effort and diligence by staff members and volunteers, as well as a keen sensitivity for human needs especially when people are most vulnerable and distressed.

4. *Tout Value:* Value is defined as "a judgment of something with respect to its worth." Parishioners are motivated to live as good stewards when they fully grasp the fact that God is the source of all we have, and simultaneously see that their grateful return of a portion of God's blessings truly makes a difference in their families, their community, and the world.

5. *Listen and Learn:* Experienced fundraisers know that they can talk so much about their organizations that donors, who were ready to contribute, suddenly change their minds. As a wise senior fundraiser observed: "The fundraiser's mission is to help donors find a match between their dreams and hopes and those of the fundraiser's

organization." This can happen only by actively listening to donors. Parish leaders must regularly solicit input and feedback from their parishioners in a way that they (the parishioners) are convinced their voices are heard.

6. *Keep Accurate Records:* One of the great donor turnoffs is poor record-keeping by a charitable organization: misspelled names, inaccurate addresses, or gift record mistakes. When an inevitable mistake occurs, the parish should not only correct it but also take great pains to "make it all right" with the parishioner.

7. *Deal Straight/Tell the Truth:* When problems and major issues arise in the parish, leaders must communicate accurate, necessary information to parishioners quickly, openly, and honestly. Recent political and religious shenanigans should provide ample evidence that denials and coverups never work. Parishioners, whose contributions of time, talent, and treasure sustain a parish, have a right to know how their contributions are being used. Furthermore, parish leaders have a weighty responsibility to be good stewards of the gifts parishioners entrust to their care. This requires astute fiscal management coupled with a disciplined, "bottom line" mentality.

8. *Say Thank You:* The two most powerful words in a fundraiser's verbal arsenal are "thank you." Gratitude must be sincere, quick to be given, and frequent. Parishioners never tire of being appropriately thanked.

9. *Offer Options:* Each parishioner's circumstances are unique. Consequently, decisions about how to make financial contributions will vary widely. A good fundraiser prepares an extensive menu of options from which parishioners can choose those which fit their situations. Parish leaders should stay abreast of current tax laws regarding charitable gifts as a protection for both the parish and its members.

10. *Stay in Touch With Donors* (professional fundraisers call this "cultivation"). Parishes need a system for keeping parishioners "in the loop" regarding all aspects of parish life. Invite parishioners to participate in developing long- and short-range strategic plans for the parish, then communicate these plans and subsequent updates to all parishioners. Personalize all correspondence as much as possible (thank God for computers!), and don't hesitate to urge people to review their stewardship of treasure regularly.

If we could add an eleventh commandment to the ten rules of sales-manship/fundraising described above, it would be LIGHTEN UP! All too often, we forget that our lives are but fleeting moments in God's eternal plan. All too often, we shackle our fundraising or stewardship of treasure efforts by taking too many things too seriously. Nothing in-spires people to greater generosity more than wit and good humor. In the words of an anonymous sage: "Rule 1: Don't sweat the small stuff. Rule 2: It's all small stuff." In Jesus' words: "Can any of you, for all his worrying, add one single cubit to his span of life?…Set your hearts on his kingdom first…and all these other things will be given you as well" (see Matthew 6:25–34).

Chicken or Egg?

There's a subtle yet passionate tug-of-war taking place between two ideo-logically distinct groups within the American Catholic stewardship conversion movement. On one end of the rope are parish and diocesan leaders who are convinced that stewardship of treasure (money) is where the action is. They believe that when parishioners are urged, taught, and/ or cajoled to give more of their hard-earned cash, a greater commit-ment of their time and talent will naturally follow. We might call this the "hearts-follow-money" approach.

At the other end of the rope are those whose feelings and biases fall on the side of stewardship of time and talent. They believe that people who are committed to a parish and truly "own" it—as demonstrated by their level of involvement—will gladly support the organization with steadily increasing financial contributions. We could refer to this as the "money-follows-hearts" viewpoint.

The debate between these two groups is a classic chicken-or-egg discourse that centers around the best way to stimulate parish stew-ardship conversion. Each group believes it possesses the key that can unlock parishioners' hearts and minds and create within them a metanoia—a rebirth, a change—to a lifestyle based on Christian stew-ardship. This author espouses the "money-follows-hearts" position, which contends that increased financial support, through fundraising activities and tithing or proportional giving programs, is directly linked to, and flows from, increased personal involvement in the life of a community. This conviction is based on overwhelming evidence accumulated from many years of observing the results of parish stewardship renewals.

Stewardship renewals are annual blocks of time—usually four to six weeks—set aside for more-intense-than-usual stewardship education and promotion. During these periods, parishes employ all available avenues of communication to heighten parishioners' awareness about the joys and benefits of adopting stewardship as a way of life. As the renewal time draws to a close, parishioners are asked to declare their intentions by filling out stewardship of treasure and/or stewardship of time and talent commitment forms.

When parishes conduct stewardship of time and talent renewals separately from stewardship of treasure renewals, a curious phenomenon inevitably occurs. The percentage of parishioners who complete and return stewardship of treasure commitment forms is substantially greater than the percentage of parishioners who complete and return time and talent forms. It seems that many of today's American Catholics are more protective of their time than their money. In other words, because they feel inordinately pressured to squeeze more and more activities into jam-packed schedules, when asked to renew their stewardship of time, talent, and treasure, Catholics are apparently more inclined to write a slightly bigger check each week, but choose not to add more demands on their time.

In their 1992 pastoral letter, *Stewardship: A Disciple's Response*, the U.S. bishops called for a stewardship conversion within the North American Catholic Church. The challenge for every parish and diocesan leader is to create a climate and a plan for this conversion among the faithful entrusted to their spiritual care. Conversion implies a change of attitude, a fresh outlook, new ways of structuring lifestyles and priorities. Simply asking parishioners to give more money, or developing more effective fundraising strategies, won't get the job done. To understand why, we must review what fundraising analysts tell us are the five top reasons why people give to charitable organizations:

1. Belief in the institution and its purposes—92 percent.
2. Belief that current needs are important—60 percent.
3. Sense of loyalty, gratitude, affection—34 percent.
4. Tax considerations—12 percent.
5. Friendship and respect for those who ask—11 percent.

Notice that most charitable giving is motivated by ownership of an organization and commitment to its mission. People who are closely connected to and engaged in their parish are aware of its needs and are much more likely than marginal members to give their financial support.

Stewardship conversion evolves over time through a wide array of activities and strategies designed to attract parishioners into the active life of the parish family. It begins with a commitment to the process by parish leaders and is based on a leadership paradigm that enables, encourages, energizes and empowers others. Parishioners are invited to participate in programs and activities that meet their spiritual and temporal needs and which make good use of their talents. When specific programs or services that are consistent with the parish's mission are not available, parishioners are urged and allowed to create them. This entire process is facilitated by clear channels of communication which includes open dialogue, active listening, and intentional planning.

Parish and diocesan leaders will know that stewardship conversion is beginning to take root when members sincerely embrace the basic stewardship tenet that all of our time, talents, and treasure are gifts from God. The quality of our stewardship and the depth of our Christian discipleship are not measured by how many of God's possessions we accumulate, but how we use God's gifts that have been entrusted to our care—particularly the most precious gifts of our time and talent.

What About Catholic Giving?

Our Sunday Visitor Press recently published a book by Charles E. Zech entitled *Why Catholics Don't Give...And What Can Be Done About It*. The book details yet another attempt to get a handle on the factors that influence Catholic giving. Among other things, Zech's research was prompted by the fact that Catholics continue to give significantly less money to support their church than do members of other religious groups.

Zech concludes his book with a chapter under the heading "Seven Things the Catholic Church Can Do to Increase Contributions." Here's a summary of his recommendations that, based on his data, he presents in descending order of impact on giving:

1. *Develop Stewardship.* "The one best thing the Church should do if it is serious about increasing giving among Catholics is to instill a sense of stewardship among its members. Stewardship must be at the center of parish life…but…must go beyond the mere raising of money. The emphases on the time and talent dimensions are at least as critical as the emphasis on treasure."

In Zech's estimation, pledging (that is, parishioners making an annual commitment to give a portion of their incomes) works better than strict tithing. He remarks: "…what does it say about a community of people who will make multi-year commitments to purchase automobiles, vacation homes, and boats, but refuse to make a yearly commitment to their church?" "People who plan their religious giving on an annual basis…contribute more."

2. *Parish Decision-Making Processes.* Zech believes his data show that "parishioners want to be consulted and have direct input into decision-making processes" and that "they want open discussion of parish issues." He writes: "One effective way of instilling a sense of stewardship in people is to develop in them an attitude of ownership of the resources over which they are stewards."

3. *Parish Size.* Although less of a drag on Catholic contributions than most other studies have alleged, Zech observes that excessively large Catholic parishes tend to rob parishioners of a sense of parish community and also increase the tendency toward free-riding. Likewise, small parishes sometimes suffer because of their inability to sustain appealing parish programs and may also allow a small clique of

parishioners to dominate parish activities. Zech concludes: "Our finding, supported by some others, is that medium-sized parishes (1,000 to 2,500 members) receive the largest contributions."

4. *Parochial Schools.* The presence of a parish school definitely impacts giving. According to Zech: "Parents who send their children to parochial schools contribute more than do other parents of school-aged children…overall, members of parishes that sponsor their own parochial school contribute more than others." He also tenders this caveat: "Whatever benefits a parish-sponsored parochial school provides are quickly dissipated when parishes merge schools." Zech recommends that "parishes that don't have a school have to find some other activity that the parish can rally around in order to generate the same sort of benefits as a school."

5. *Teachings.* Zech's findings suggest that some Catholic teachings have been shown to have a greater impact on giving than others. One of these is the message of ecumenism. Parishioners who disagree with the notion that only followers of Jesus can be saved contribute more. Another factor associated with larger giving concerns the primary duty of Christians. Zech says: "Here, two separate themes stood out as attracting greater contributions. One was an emphasis on Church traditions and sacraments…the other teaching was concerned with changing unjust social structures." For example, Zech notes that those who support the Church's position on abortion and birth control are better givers (contrary to the personal opinion expressed by Andrew Greeley in conjunction with his earlier research on Catholic giving). On the other hand, those who disagree with the Church's position on the ordination of women also contribute more.

6. **Remind People That the Church Needs Their Contributions.** Zech states: "…many Catholics believe that their church is wealthy and doesn't need their financial support.…The fact of the matter is that the Church does need our contributions to maintain itself and to expand its ministries. Catholics who believe that the Church has serious financial needs contribute more."

7. *Meet the Special Needs of Parishioners.* "Parishes need to stand ready to meet (diverse) needs," says Zech. He believes that Generation X-ers, in particular, need special attention. They want a high level of

involvement in parish decision-making processes, they are more likely to believe in the primacy of individual conscience over Church teachings (It's more important to be a good Christian than it is to be a good Catholic.), and they feel less of an obligation to support their church financially. And, finally, another group that warrants special attention are the adult parishioners who do not have children living at home. They are often forgotten as parishes gear their programs and resources toward children.

Money Talks

From time to time, in every parish, circumstances dictate the need to talk about money. On one such occasion, as the pastor began a homily about money, a parishioner leaned toward his wife and whispered: "Uh oh, here comes another sermon on the amount!"

Any mention of money during Mass triggers a wide variety of sentiments. Guilt, anger, embarrassment, and self-righteous indignation would probably summarize the reactions of many parishioners. In fact, when the topic of money is broached in church, one would often be hard pressed to find many faces that identify Saint Paul's "cheerful giver[s]" (2 Corinthians 9:7) who are convinced it is "more blessed to give than to receive" (Acts 20:35).

Every reference to Christian stewardship should automatically bring to mind the classic three Ts: Time, Talent, and Treasure. Each element of this stewardship trinity, much like the Holy Trinity in Catholic theology, is equally significant. However, in the real parish world of bills, buildings, and payrolls, stewardship of treasure sometimes becomes "more equal" than its two companions. In recognition of this reality, let's review some of the factors and issues that impact the stewardship of treasure within a parish setting.

Each year, the Giving USA Foundation, a Trust for Philanthropy of the American Association of Fundraising Counsel (AAFRC), publishes a fascinating book entitled *Giving USA*. Here are a few facts taken from the most recent issue (2005), regarding charitable giving for 2004:

1. Total charitable giving in the United States increased by 5 percent from 2003 to 2004, from $236.7 billion to $248.5 billion (page ii).
2. Giving to religious congregations and denominations during that same period increased by 4.4 percent, to $88.3 billion. Religious giving amounts to about 35.5 percent of the total allocated charitable giving, and is, by far, the largest slice of the U.S. philanthropic pie (page 16). Other "pie-pieces" include education, health, human services, arts/culture/humanities, gifts to foundations, public/society benefit, environment/wildlife, and international affairs.
3. Church giving by Catholics continues to lag behind Protestant giving. "Sixty-five percent of all adults contributed to a church or other place of worship in 2004. The average gift was $895 per donor. Evangelicals reported giving an average of $3,250 to the their churches…whereas other Protestants gave an average of $1,304, and Catholics gave an average of $547 to their churches" (page 100).

Many diocesan stewardship directors anecdotally report that parishes that commit to a process of total stewardship conversion experience substantial increases in financial support. But tithing, proportional giving, or sacrificial giving models are still not fully embraced in most U.S. parishes. We know that many Catholics give generously, but only when certain conditions are met such as a likable pastor, a demonstrated, particular need, or children enrolled in the parish school. This pattern of "giving-to-need" suggests the presence of a purchase of services or "pay-the-bills" mentality rather than giving that is prompted by a stewardship way of life. (More about this later.)

Following a particularly contentious meeting of the presbyterate in one diocese, a pastor remarked: "Trying to get a group of priests to agree on something is like trying to herd cats!" There is, however, one thing upon which most priests will readily agree: talking about money is distasteful, at best. The reasons for this aversion are numerous; for some, it's guilt—conscious or subconscious—about their own lifestyles; for others, it's lack of training and experience in the fundamentals of stewardship and fundraising; for still others, it may be a lingering misunderstanding about the theology of money fueled by the mistaken perception that money is "filthy lucre" (see below). Regardless of the source of this dislike for "talking money," more education for pastoral leaders about financial matters and stewardship is clearly needed.

Does this formula sound familiar: Money = Profits = Business = Greed = Injustice = Evil? It's an equation that seems to be activated in the psyches of many people when money is mentioned within a religious context. To be sure, there is some basis for this reaction. One can indeed find unscrupulous, greedy, unjust people in the business world. However, we are frequently and painfully reminded by the news media that religious leaders are not immune from the sin of greed, or any other sin for that matter!

Objectively, we know that money is nothing more than pieces of paper and metal we have agreed to use as a means of exchange. The viewpoint that money is somehow obscene is often fueled by a misquotation of a New Testament passage that has become one of the hackneyed saws of the English language: "Money is the root of all evil." The actual verse in 1 Timothy is: "...*the love of money* is root of all kinds of evil" (6:10, emphasis added).

Money is a tool, an instrument; as such, it is amoral. Money is also another gift from a good and generous God. How we, as disciples of Jesus Christ, use God's gifts, including money, will be the focus of our ultimate stewardship performance review at the Final Judgment.

As mentioned above, many Catholics seem to operate from a "give-to-need" frame of mind rather than from a stewardship-based "need-to-give" mode. An astute pastor recently characterized the give-to-need attitude as a "pay-the-bills mentality." Pay-the-bills thinking works like this: when the collection basket is passed, PTB parishioners toss in a check or cash, loose or inside a contribution envelope, the amount of which is often determined by how they feel that day or what they happen to have in their purse or wallet. PTB-ers give from a sense of duty or obligation. They can be quite generous, but only when they are convinced of a specific need, approve of the pastor, and are asked to give.

Giving the steward's way, on the other hand, is a grateful and joyful return of a portion of God's property that is temporarily on loan to us. Good stewards give just for the sake of giving. They base their philanthropy on tithing or proportional giving. Rather than "giving-to-need," good stewards recognize a "need-to-give," without being asked, and often with little concern about how their gifts will be used.

What we might conclude from all of the above is that we still have much work to do in Catholic parishes and dioceses to achieve the conversion to stewardship called for by the U.S. bishops in their pastoral letter, *Stewardship: A Disciple's Response.* But we know that the Holy Spirit is guiding our efforts, so how can we fail?

STEP 7

Accountability

Success in the stewardship and development efforts of a parish or diocese requires a visible commitment to accountability. This commitment includes accountability for the full range of parish or diocesan activities—from the way decisions are made and carried out by diocesan or parish personnel to the way money is collected, managed, and used. Indeed, **accountability is fundamental to good stewardship** *[emphasis added].*

Parishes and dioceses are urged to prepare annual reports of their stewardship. These reports should be prepared in a manner that promotes understanding of the relationship between the ministries of the Church and the financial affairs of the parish or diocese. Church leaders should also use the annual report to render an account of their stewardship of human resources (personnel policies [or] just compensations), and their stewardship of church property and facilities.

A visible commitment to accountability will be reflected in the leadership styles and attitudes of the bishop, pastor, and all who have responsibilities for the human, physical, and financial resources of the diocese or parish. Like personal witness, a commitment to accountability is essential to building a solid foundation for a diocesan or parish stewardship program.

STEWARDSHIP: A DISCIPLE'S RESPONSE (PAGE 61)

You Might Be a Good Steward If...

It may sound old-fashioned, but Christians still profess to believe that there will be a Final Judgment for each human being, and for mankind as a whole. God, the final arbiter, will tell us if our earthly behavior and intentions have merited the eternal rewards that Christ promised.

However, just as employees don't like to receive "you're terminated" pink slips with no prior indications of any problems, most reasonable Christians would, from time to time, like to know how they're doing as disciples of Jesus Christ. Therefore, we offer the following self-assessment checklist—not divinely inspired!—as a tool for Christians to evaluate their progress on their stewardship journey.

You might be a good steward if…

You sincerely believe God is the source of all your blessings.

You feel a need to return a portion of your blessings to God out of gratitude.

You understand that stewardship is not an option but an obligation for disciples of Jesus.

You're not afraid to model good stewardship to others.

You joyfully return a fair measure of God's gifts, expecting nothing in return.

You try to attend Mass more than once a week.

You've made the scriptural tithe (giving back to God 10 percent of your time, talent, and treasure) a goal for your life; you've either reached that goal or are moving toward it through proportional giving.

You view good stewardship as a happy responsibility flowing from God's gift of faith, not as a nuisance or inconvenience.

Your generosity is proportional: it increases with your blessings and resources.

You feel a duty to care for ALL of God's creations.

You accept your Christian call to be hospitable and welcoming to everyone you meet.

You actively seek opportunities to share your time, talent, and treasure; you rarely have to be prompted to help or volunteer.

You cherish celebrating the Eucharist, and spending time with your fellow believers.

You don't worry about what you will eat, drink or wear; you "strive first for the kingdom of God" (Matthew 6:31–33).

You teach your children and others to be good stewards by your word and example.

You are convinced that God cannot be outdone in generosity.

You are a blessed peacemaker in all of your relationships.

You are sincerely trying to live the definition of a Christian steward from the U.S. Bishops' 1992 pastoral letter, *Stewardship: A Disciple's Response:* Christian steward is "one who receives God's gifts gratefully, cherishes and tends them in a responsible and accountable manner, shares them in justice and love with others, and returns them with increase to the Lord" (page 9).

If most of these attributes describe you and your fellow parishioners, your progress toward a stewardship way of life, and that of your parish, is moving in the right direction. You can reasonably assume that God is pleased. Keep up the good work!

How Are We Doing?

During a recent meeting of a diocesan committee reviewing the compensation package for priests, one of the lay volunteer committee members, a highly regarded local corporate executive, innocently suggested that a portion of clergy compensation be tied to measurable performance criteria. The response from the clergy members of the committee was swift and unequivocal: such an idea was preposterous. Their objection was that priests perform such a wide array of functions that there would be no way to develop uniform measures of accountability. As one priest committee member put it: "Nobody knows all the things I do."

The corporate executive was somewhat taken aback by the priests' strong negative reaction to his suggestion. In his professional, bottom-line-oriented business world, evaluation and accountability are "givens"— they're simply components of the system. The impact on a company of either positive or negative evaluations by customers and investors can be profound. In the late 1990s, flash-in-the-pan "dot com" millionaires were reminded of a fundamental lesson in business accountability: a for-profit organization's ultimate measure of success is quite simple: the company's either profitable or it's not. If it makes money, it survives; if it doesn't, it perishes.

There's no question that accountability and evaluation are potentially fearful words. For some, these words conjure up images of cold-hearted corporations forcing employees to produce more and more products with no regard for the consequences, or micro-managerial control-freaks hovering over workers waiting to catch them making a mistake. However, when used appropriately, accountability and evaluation can be powerful tools for positively motivating employees and improving a company's performance and profitability.

It's important to realize that evaluation and accountability also exist in the nonprofit world, which includes religious organizations, albeit less systematically than in the business community. Catholic parishioners, for example, constantly evaluate their parishes and dioceses. Their assessments often result in dramatic consequences. Based on their appraisals, people join parishes and leave parishes; people support parishes or they don't; people choose to share their time and talent or they don't; people attend Mass regularly or they don't. All of these are legitimate measures of the success or failure of a parish community.

One of the most important features of a total stewardship parish should be its willingness to engage in an endeavor we might refer to as "proactive accountability." Proactive accountability is based on the belief that organizations are never perfect. They can always do a better job no matter what. Proactive accountability begins with parish leaders publicly declaring their desire to make theirs the best possible parish, then establishing a user-friendly system of continuous feedback that engages all parishioners.

In practice, proactive accountability involves parish leaders continuously posing a series of questions about the status of the conduct and activities of the parish: How are we doing as a parish? What do we do well? What do we need to improve? What do we need to discontinue or add? What are our goals? Do we have benchmarks to measure progress toward our goals?

Parish stewardship conversion is a never-ending process that hinges on parish leaders' obsession with perfection. Practically everything that takes place in a parish can be done more efficiently or more effectively: prayer life and liturgies, welcoming and hospitality, business administration, programs and services, and so on. How is your parish doing?

A Cut Above

In every two-way human relationship, including the one between parishioner and parish, both parties maintain something we'll call a Personal Relationship Scorecard (PRS). A parish's PRS usually includes such tangible items as church attendance, offertory contributions, participation in activities, and children who attend parish school. A parishioner's PRS is primarily a mental checklist of items such as the length of sermons, quality of liturgical music, friendliness of pastor and staff, parish hospitality, quality of parish school, availability of a priest when needed, services/programs that meet my needs, and so on.

Over time, it's the little things, the daily grind that causes relationships to either thrive or turn sour. When, for example, the negative entries on a parishioner's PRS begin to outnumber the positive marks, the parishioner begins to think about moving to another parish, or another denomination, or simply quitting "church" all together.

Why do some parishes consistently earn higher PRS marks than others? Here's a clue from your own experiences to help you answer that question. When you have occasion to attend Mass in other parishes, don't you notice differences? Yes, the basic liturgical elements are the same, but the ambience and spirit of Catholic parish communities often vary widely. You recognize, from your own travels, that some parish communities are simply a cut above the rest.

What is it that separates average parishes from outstanding ones? Great parish communities seem to understand and practice a principle that the business world refers to as "value-added." Simply stated, value-added means going above and beyond what one would normally expect.

Here's a sampling of the things one would expect to find in an average Catholic parish, followed by their value-added counterparts in a "cut-above" parish:

One would expect homilies to be well-prepared. Value-added homilies are memorized and delivered with conviction and passion.

One would expect greeters at Mass to smile and say, "Good morning." Value-added greeters not only welcome each person to the parish but also make a special effort to identify visitors and parish newcomers. In fact, in a great parish, *every* parishioner is a minister of hospitality, not just those who wear "Greeter" name tags.

One would expect necessary arrangements for all parish-sponsored meetings and activities (clean room, clear signage, proper equipment, or punctual start times). Value-added parishes provide appropriate refreshments and childcare for every gathering.

Newcomers to a parish would expect a "welcome to the parish" letter from the pastor and information about parish activities and programs. In a value-added parish, the pastor, a staff member, or a "welcome committee" volunteer personally visits the homes of new members to welcome them to the parish and may even take them to lunch or dinner.

One would expect a visit from the pastor or pastoral associate when in the hospital. In value-added parishes, parish staff members or volunteers visit the parishioner at home during his or her recovery period and provide whatever help they can.

Get the idea? If you want a quick read on how your parish scores on parishioners' PRSs, ask newcomers and visitors to share their first impressions about your parish. Their reactions and comments will tell you if your parish is in the "cut-above" class or if you still have some work to do to become a true stewardship parish community of prayer, hospitality, and service.

Another Fad Fades

Another fashion craze has come and gone. Each time it happens, most of us react with nothing more than a routine "ho-hum." But the passing of this particular phenomenon has been markedly disheartening for many idealistic Christians.

Not long ago, it was considered "cool" by some teens and young adults to wear bracelets and articles of clothing with the letters WWJD printed on them. The letters are the abbreviation for "What Would Jesus Do?" For those of us who are spiritual romantics, the WWJD fad filled our hearts with hopeful excitement. We secretly rejoiced each time we encountered people wearing those meaningful letters. It was particularly inspiring to observe young people attempting to make WWJD the backdrop for their developing values and personal behavior.

For a brief period, we allowed ourselves to imagine a world where the sentiment of WWJD drove all human interaction, where societies use WWJD as the basis for their constitutional ideologies, and where parishes unswervingly approach their prayer lives, service delivery systems, and hospitality efforts from a WWJD perspective! It was exhilarating!

However, in the realistic recesses of our psyches, we knew the WWJD phenomenon was just another fleeting historical episode. In fact, WWJD items are now difficult to find. But the lifestyle advocated by the WWJD sensation is not only still absolutely valid, it's supremely appropriate for people and parishes committed to stewardship conversion.

The U.S. bishops opened their 1992 pastoral letter on stewardship with this declaration: "The Christian vocation is essentially a call to be a disciple of Jesus" (page 13). Later in the document, they wrote: "Whoever wants to follow Christ will have much work to do on his behalf— announcing the good news and serving others as Jesus did….Becoming a disciple of Jesus Christ leads naturally to the practice of stewardship" (page 14). The official summary of the pastoral, entitled "To Be a Christian steward" ended with these words: "Central to our human and Christian vocations, as well as to the unique vocation each one of us receives from God, is that we be good stewards of the gifts we possess. God gives us this divine-human workshop, this world and Church of ours. The Spirit shows us the way. Stewardship is part of that journey."

The bishops could not have been clearer: discipleship and stewardship are two sides of the same Christian coin. Stewardship is, in fact, the means by which we demonstrate our discipleship. In practical terms, being a good steward/disciple of Jesus Christ includes constantly invoking WWJD as a tool for monitoring our attitudes and actions.

Establishing a general WWJD attitude within a parish family must begin with a declaration of intent by the pastor, pastoral staff, and key parish leaders. The purpose of this public announcement is to alert all parishioners that, from this day forward, everything we say and do, both as a parish community and as individual Catholic disciples of Jesus Christ, will flow from a WWJD frame of reference.

Consider for a moment the numerous classes, committee meetings, social gatherings, study groups, and assemblies of clubs and organizations in every parish where ideas are discussed, attitudes are displayed, opinions are expressed, and decisions are made. When a parish espouses a WWJD philosophy, it automatically places all of its operations within a WWJD framework as a tool for evaluating every idea, opinion, and decision.

How can a parish ensure the effectiveness of its WWJD infrastructure? One excellent means is by creating a WWJD Overseers Program. WWJD Overseers are designated individuals who, with appropriate training, serve as a WWJD conscience whenever parishioners come together in Christ's name. When, during the course of a parish gathering, a decision must be made or a controversy must be resolved, the WWJD Overseer is empowered to intervene by actually saying the words: "In this instance, what would Jesus do?" then asking the group to pause for a moment of silent reflection and prayer before moving toward a final decision or conflict resolution. Imagine the centering power of this intervention, especially when a discussion is heated, when a decision is painful, or when a consensus seems impossible!

Here are a few circumstances which might trigger the need for a WWJD Overseer's intervention:

- During a religious education class for high-school students, the discussion turns to the pros and cons of premarital sex.
- A parish council is asked to advise the pastor regarding whether to allow smoking and drinking of alcohol in parish buildings.
- A parish finance committee reviews the wages for parish employees as it prepares the following year's budget.
- A handful of disgruntled parents complains to a parish school board that the behavior standards in the parish school are too strict for their children.
- A parish social club, which has operated as an exclusive group for many years, considers including new members from different ethnic groups which have recently moved into the parish.
- A St. Vincent de Paul organization discusses whether to put most of its money into investments or give it to the poor.
- A strategic planning committee tries to set long-range parish goals that will significantly impact current and future programs and services.
- A parish stewardship committee questions whether or not to continue gambling activities as major means of support for the parish school and other programs.
- A parish liturgy committee considers ways to improve parish liturgical celebrations that require changing from "the way we've always done it."

Although we see fewer and fewer WWJD items in department stores and boutiques these days, we are still obligated, as Christ's disciples, to be good stewards of God's many gifts to us. Yes, another fad has passed, but its compelling message endures.

Is Your Parish Ready for Stewardship Conversion?

Promoting a stewardship way of life is a practice that is most certainly gaining a foothold within the Catholic Church in North America. More and more dioceses and parishes have accepted the U.S. bishops' challenge, as expressed in their 1992 pastoral letter, *Stewardship: A Disciple's Response,* to engage in a process of stewardship conversion. As mentioned earlier, Catholics are beginning to realize that stewardship is not a "Protestant thing" nor is it simply a euphemism for fundraising.

However, even as the message of stewardship continues to spread, we've already noted that many Catholics still have not embraced the three fundamental principles upon which Christian stewardship is based:

1. Everything we are and have belongs to God.
2. We should be enormously grateful for all of our God-given gifts and use them responsibly.
3. Out of gratitude, we need to share a portion of our gifts of time, talent, and treasure as an expression of our discipleship in Jesus Christ.

It's increasingly obvious that the success of the stewardship movement depends on each parish's ability to create an atmosphere that is conducive to a radical stewardship *metanoia*—a change of heart—among its members. There are numerous clues that a parish is ripe for a process of stewardship conversion. Here are a few of those clues expressed in remarks often overheard in some parishes:

- "Nobody around here wants to do anything. It's always the same few people who do all the work!"
- "Going to Mass here is such a drag!"
- "All they ever talk about in this parish is money."

- "If you don't get to Mass at least a half-hour early on Christmas and Easter, be prepared to stand in the parking lot."
- "It's so difficult to find out what's going on in this parish."
- "Whatever happened to those RCIA folks who were baptized and confirmed last year?"
- "You can never find a priest when you need one."
- "Can anyone remember the last time a deceased parishioner left something to the parish in his or her will?"
- "Does anyone know where to find a copy of the strategic plan we adopted two years ago?"
- "I'll gladly help with (name of activity here), but don't ever ask me to be in charge of it—or anything else, for that matter."
- "Have you noticed that there are fewer and fewer young families at Mass each week?"
- "This parish could never survive without its weekly bingo games."
- "No one really seems to care about all the time and effort volunteers put into this parish."
- "I see new people at Mass for three or four weeks in a row and then they just seem to disappear."

Do any of these comments sound familiar when you think of your parish? Each one highlights issues that could be addressed effectively by a renewed commitment to good stewardship. And there's no time like the present to get started.

A Generic Vision for Parish Stewardship

Let's assume that your parish's stewardship conversion ducks have all been aligned: the pastor has expressed a passionate desire for the congregation to embrace a stewardship way of life; the parish council has given its enthusiastic endorsement; a competent, zealous stewardship committee has been selected and is prepared to lead the parish to total stewardship. What's next?

The next step is to develop some type of "Vision Statement," which is a formal, public declaration of the parish's commitment to a process of stewardship conversion and a description of what the parish hopes to become. Parish leaders, stewardship committee members and parishioners will own the process and be much more effective if they have a clear sense of direction and a destination for the stewardship journey that lies ahead.

A good vision statement for parish stewardship conversion should reflect the personality of the parish. It should inspire and motivate as well as give direction and purpose. Above all, it should be useful and practical. Organizations have been known to spend countless hours crafting lengthy, "perfect" vision statements with catchy words and clever phrases. Yet many of these masterpieces ultimately wind up in a file folder or hang on a wall somewhere in a frame that serves as a dust collector.

Someone once observed that truly great vision and mission statements can be comfortably printed on a T-shirt. They consist of a short phrase or two that conveys a message that is both straightforward and dynamic. With this in mind, I'd like to recommend a generic vision statement for stewardship conversion. This statement captures the essence of stewardship conversion in a few simple words and can be used by any parish (or diocese) to describe its dream goal of total stewardship. Best of all, it can be adapted to fit easily on a T-shirt.

My suggestion for a universally applicable vision statement for stewardship conversion is: "To make (Name of Parish here) the best possible parish." That's it; no frills; no nonsense; no literary smoke and mirrors. A T-shirt-size adaptation would be something like: "(Name) Parish: Excellence in Ministry."

This powerful little statement conveys a multitude of messages about the parish:

- We will not "settle." We will never be satisfied with anything less than the best.
- We will search incessantly for more and better ways to recognize and appreciate God's gifts of time, talent, and treasure.
- We will be tireless in showing parishioners that their parish truly cares about them in good times and bad.

- We are dedicated to developing the best possible religious education programs, liturgical celebrations, works of charity and social justice, hospitality and welcoming initiatives, evangelization and reconciliation efforts, spiritual development, compassionate ministries, and so on.

Notice that the statement does *not* say "*the best* parish" or "*the Number One* parish." Stewardship conversion is not a contest with other parishes. The expressed dream is that your parish is constantly striving for excellence in everything it does, just as every other parish should be working to reach its full potential. Any sense of competition should only involve the parish competing with itself.

The impossible dream, expressed above in the generic vision statement, is perfection in every aspect of parish life—a goal that will never be attained. However, being good stewards of God's gifts means being accountable for them and productive with them. *Striving* for perfection is, or should be, one of the hallmarks of disciples of Jesus Christ. What still needs some work and attention in your parish?

Postscript
Stewardship: Yes or No?

This book contains several dozen essays that touch on nearly every aspect of Christian stewardship and the parish stewardship conversion process. For the most part, the reflections consist of philosophical or theological nuances about stewardship, or practical strategies for increasing parishioners' offerings of time, talent, and treasure. In this final essay, I'm going to "cut to the chase." Based on years of empirical observations, I've chosen to reveal the single, nearly miraculous ingredient that creates a successful stewardship parish.

I begin my revelation by posing a simple question: "Why does stewardship conversion seem to take root and flourish in some parishes and not in others?" What is the fundamental stimulus that turns an ordinary parish community into active disciples of Jesus Christ who accept ownership of their parish and embrace stewardship as a way of life? I submit that successful parish stewardship conversion boils down to the two most powerful words in any language: *Yes* and *No*.

Each of us has experienced the impact of these two words time and again in our lives, especially when they're spoken by someone with authority and power. Hearing the word *yes* can produce a wave of exhilarating, liberating emotions: "Yes, you may go to the movies." "Yes, you can use the family car." "Yes, I will marry you." The Virgin Mary's "yes" changed the course of history. Jesus, the eternal yes, overcame the power of death for all mankind. But *yes* can also be alarming and destructive: "Yes, you can drink alcohol when your high-school friends come over." To an unwed teenager: "Yes, you're pregnant." "Yes, you have cancer."

Likewise, the word *no* can produce both positive and negative affective and behavioral consequences. Saying no to something that is dangerous, illegal, unethical, or immoral is obviously a good thing. On the other hand, repeatedly hearing "no" to suggestions, ideas, and recommendations made by members of a community sincerely trying to make a difference will stifle their creativity, destroy their motivation, and eventually demoralize them.

When it comes to parish stewardship conversion, there are only two types of parishes: "Yes-Parishes," where stewardship thrives, and "No-Parishes," where stewardship fails. Yes-Parishes cultivate a positive "Yes! Culture" beginning with a formal public commitment to the process of stewardship conversion by the pastor, staff members, and influential parish leaders. In a Yes-Parish, leaders model good stewardship and are willing to do whatever it takes, within reason, to move the parish toward its goal of total stewardship. Yes-Parishes encourage risk-taking. Leaders and parishioners are allowed to make mistakes, provided they learn from them. They are willing to try new things. They welcome feedback and fresh ideas, and celebrate diversity and creativity. Yes-Parishes are constantly on the lookout for ways to improve their hospitality, prayer life, and services. Yes-Parishes are ALIVE! with an accountable, can-do attitude. Each day begins by asking: "How can we become better disciples of Jesus Christ today?"

By contrast, No-Parishes are controlled by an intimidating, systematic "No! Culture." Their leaders are skilled in the use of phrases that the business world calls "idea killers" such as: "We tried that before," "Our parish is different," "We're too busy," "It costs too much," "It's not my style," "That's just the way I am," "We've never done it before," "I don't like the idea," "We're not ready for that," "It won't work here," "It's too much trouble," "We've always done it this way," "There's not enough help," and the insidious "You're right, but…"

So, when it comes to stewardship conversion in your parish or diocese—and in your life—what's it going to be: Yes or No?

Bibliography

A Shepherd's Care: Reflections on the Changing Role of Pastor. Bishops' Committee on Priestly Life and Ministry. Washington, DC: National Conference of Catholic Bishops, 1987.

A Time to Listen...A Time to Heal. Committee on Evangelization of the United States Conference of Catholic Bishops. Washington, DC: United States Catholic Conference, 1999.

Clements, C. Justin. *Stewardship: A Parish Handbook.* Liguori, Mo.: Liguori Publications, 2000.

Clements, C. Justin. *The Steward's Way.* Kansas City, Mo.: Sheed & Ward, 1997.

Cousins, Norman. *Anatomy of an Illness as Perceived by the Patient.* New York: Norton, 1979.

Covey, Stephen. *The Seven Habits of Highly Effective People.* New York: Simon & Schuster, 1989.

Deming, W. Edwards. *Out of the Crisis.* Cambridge, Mass.: MIT, 1982.

Giving USA. AAFRC Trust for Philanthropy. Bloomington, Ind.: The Center on Philanthropy at Indiana University, 2005.

Go and Make Disciples—Tenth Anniversary Edition. Committee on Evangelization of the National Conference of Catholic Bishops. Washington, DC: USCCB, 2002.

Greenleaf, Robert K. Essay: *The Servant as Leader* (1970). (*The Power of Servant-Leadership.* Editor, Larry C. Spears. San Francisco: Berrett-Koehler Publishers, 1998.)

Jones, Laurie Beth. *Jesus CEO.* New York: Hyperion, 1995.

Nash, Ogden. Speech delivered at granddaughter's 1970 high school graduation. *The Atlantic Monthly*, June–July 2002.

Stewardship : A Disciple's Response—Tenth Anniversary Edition. Committee on Stewardship of the United States Conference of Catholic Bishops. Washington, DC: USCCB, 2002.

The Reluctant Steward. Indianapolis, Ind.: Lilly Endowment, Inc., 1992.

The Reluctant Steward Revisited. Indianapolis, Ind.: Lilly Endowment, Inc., 2002.

Zech, Charles. *Why Catholic Don't Give and What Can Be Done About It.* Huntington, Ind.: Our Sunday Visitor Press, 2000.